ENAMELLING

ENAMELLING

RUTH BALL

HERBERT PRESS
LONDON • OXFORD • NEW YORK • NEW DELHI • SYDNEY

HERBERT PRESS
Bloomsbury Publishing Plc
50 Bedford Square, London, WC1B 3DP, UK
29 Earlsfort Terrace, Dublin 2, Ireland

BLOOMSBURY, HERBERT PRESS and the Herbert Press logo are trademarks of
Bloomsbury Publishing Plc

First published in 2006 by Bloomsbury Publishing Plc
Reprinted 2012, 2016, 2018, 2022

British Library Cataloguing-in-Publication Data
A catalogue record for this book is available from the British Library.

ISBN: PB: 978-1-912217-45-8

Book design by Jo Tapper
Cover design by Sutchinda Rangsi Thompson
Copyedited by Rebecca Harman
Proofread by Julian Beecroft
Project Manager: Susan Kelly
Index: Sophie Page

Printed and bound in India by Replika Press Pvt. Ltd.

MIX
Paper from
responsible sources
FSC® C016779
FSC
www.fsc.org

To find out more about our authors and books visit www.bloomsbury.com and sign up for our
newsletters.

*Frontispiece: Necklace by Ruth Rushby. Enamel, silver, 18-carat and fine gold detail.
Photo: Joel Degen*

CONTENTS

ACKNOWLEDGEMENTS

For Graham, Matthew and Laura

My greatest thanks to all the contributors to this book, who have given much support and generously allowed their images to be used. Special thanks to personal friends and professional colleagues who have continuously given encouragement, help and advice. Deepest gratitude to all my former tutors, who have been so inspirational, developing my interest in art, design, jewellery-making and, most importantly, enamel. Finally, complete and total thanks to my family for their patience, kindness and love.

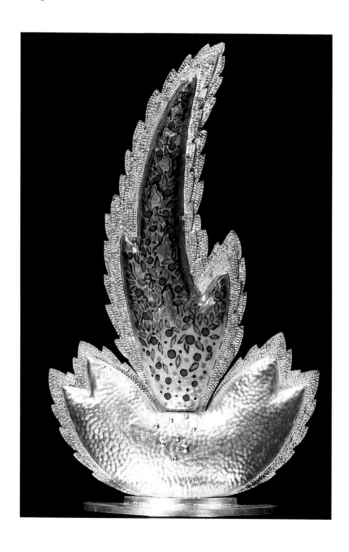

INTRODUCTION

Enamel is the reward of patience. It is an intensive process, with immensely satisfying results.

Enamel in itself does not have any intrinsic value. It is merely glass fused to metal. However, at its best it can render a piece priceless with its unique characteristics and sheer beauty. As a medium it can be used across a wide variety of formats. It can embellish a tiny jewel or ultimately become an architectural-scale artwork that will cover an entire wall.

In social terms, enamel has infiltrated diverse spheres of life. Enamelled jewellery and objets d'art, fashioned for the opulent pleasure of kings and nobility, are well recognised. Humble forms of adornment awarded for service or achievement are equally treasured. The medal, the badge or even simple buttons may show their special splash of colour.

The remarkable range of effects that can be achieved in enamel are infinite. It not only offers the jeweller limitless colour possibilities, but can also provide many subtleties of surface and a range of textures. It has the ability to enhance form and has the power to mesmerise.

With the emphasis on contemporary design and modern methods, the aim of this book is to explain the different techniques and show the diversity of enamel. Predominantly, the focus is on items of jewellery, but included are examples of small objects, tableware, sculpture and panels, to display the wider opportunities for creative development.

In addition to the technical information, work by British and international enamellists reveal pieces that are inspirational. The variety of contemporary styles provides a glimpse of what is attainable. The creative thinking, individuality and skill of the enamellists selected reflect the overall energy and dedication of those involved in current contemporary practice.

My own fascination is that each enamellist will have a different approach to the medium. Given the same materials, the results become so individual, each person developing their own distinctive aspect. The breadth of possibility is matched only by the limits of the enamellist's imagination.

Ornamental paisley perfume vessel *by Ruth Ball, 1989. Painted enamel on silver. 10 x 5.5cm (4 x 2¼ in.). Photo: Ruth Ball*

Painted enamel portrait of Admiral Lord Nelson by Gillie Hoyte Byrom.
Enamel on 18-carat gold. Photo: Alan Cooper Labs

CHAPTER ONE

HISTORY, SAFETY AND EQUIPMENT

A BRIEF HISTORY

Contemporary enamellists have the foundation of a rich heritage from which to study, absorb and glean knowledge. Enamel, in existence over the past three millennia, has been a constant attraction for jewellers and silversmiths, offering alluring possiblities for colouring objects and adding emphasis to designs.

Enamel traditions have foundations in many countries. Historical events, social changes and the initiation of trade routes led to a number of geographical areas becoming notable centres of excellence.

My Enamelled Medals, *Marilyn Druin, 1993. Enamel on silver with gold details. 8 x 2.5 cm (3¹/₃ x 1 in.). Photo: Mel Druin*

The earliest examples of enamel artefacts date from the Mycenaean period. Enamelling later flourished at the time of the Byzantine Empire, and under Ottoman rule pieces emanated from Persia. In later periods, workshops prevailed in several European countries, most notably in Germany, France and Italy. Russian enamel evolved in succeeding eras, as did Asian, Chinese, Indian and Japanese enamels. Each highly cultivated civilisation independently added to the development and evolution of the technique, thus enriching the legacy of enamel methods.

Over time, through the meeting of cultures and the growth in knowledge, different methods of fusing enamel to metal were formulated. However, the main techniques, namely *cloisonné*, *champlevé*, *plique à jour* and painted enamel, have prevailed since ancient times.

Enamel has typically mirrored the fashions each century, resulting in many differences in style and technique. For instance, medieval works devoted themselves to religious themes dictated by the Church, whilst the artists of the Renaissance period sought more representational and richly decorated wares. The most prolific era for enamelling was the Art Nouveau period. Enamellers skilfully embraced the stylised forms of the time and became absorbed in the ethos of the movement.

The inheritance of imagery and forms from the Art Nouveau period is still in evidence today. The eternal themes of beauty and nature hold strong. At the highest level of skill, enamellers continue to produce examples of enamel that equal the work of the past. In contemporary works, however, the emphasis is on innovation and design. It is in the mastery of enamel's diverse techniques that enamel is pushed forward, but, most importantly, it is in the spirit of an innovative approach to design that enamel has its future.

Abstract brooch by Ros Conway, 1985.
Approx. 6 x 4.5 cm (2¹/₃ x 1¹/₄ in.).
Enamel on silver, made in collaboration
with painter Hugh O'Donnell.
Collection: Dr Carolyn Watkins.
Photo: Ros Conway

HEALTH AND SAFETY

Enamelling is a safe and rewarding activity, but there are also safety considerations, and a common sense approach should be employed in order to protect yourself against possible risks. Basic care is needed to guard against the potential effects of dust, and to control the heat and the fumes. Extreme care is needed if you use chemicals.

General points

- All work areas should be kept tidy and free from any obstructions.
- Good ventilation in your workshop is essential.
- You should wear a dust/fume mask if using the enamels dry, and keep areas free of dust.
- Clothing should be kept tidy, i.e. no long scarves, long sleeves or items that could get caught in equipment.
- Keep long hair tied back.
- Safety goggles/face visor should be worn when engraving or using machinery.
- You may need specialist UV glasses if you are firing enamels for long periods.
- Kilns and trivets will get very hot, so always wear heat-resistant gloves when firing work. Use tweezers to handle pieces.

Safety equipment: goggles, gloves and dust mask

- A glass brush should always be used under running water. The fibres in the brush are very fine and can irritate the skin. Always brush away from yourself and wear protective gloves.
- Equipment should be used with care, following the manufacturer's guidelines, and should always be well maintained.
- If you use acids, you should always wear full safety clothing (rubber gloves, safety goggles, safety apron and solid footwear) and must only work in supervised, specialist facilities with full ventilation.

Lead in enamel

Enamels can be bought with or without lead content. All lead-bearing enamels carry toxicity/poison symbols, as they contain lead and hazardous compounds. Unleaded enamels carry the harmful/irritant symbol.

As with any lead-bearing material, there are safety measures to be considered. Lead is potentially harmful. With regard to enamel the exposure risks are linked to dust and fumes. The health hazards when using enamel depend on the level of exposure and the method of control.

There is little risk involved unless enamel powder enters the body, risks can be minimised by safe working practice. Lead can be absorbed into your body by inhalation (breathing) or ingestion (eating).

It is unlikely that you will want to eat your enamel, but you must ensure that you do not eat, drink or smoke in your workshop so as to minimise any contamination from enamel particles. You should always wash your hands after handling enamel.

The most likely occupational hazard is breathing in the enamel as dust or fumes. Therefore, you should only enamel in a well-ventilated area, exercise vigilant dust control and wear a suitable dust mask.

As a precaution, if you are using enamel in a group or educational setting, particularly with children, unleaded enamels are preferable in terms of health and safety. You must still follow procedures for dust control. If you are working in an industrial setting you should seek advice from your health and safety officer. If you consider that you are (or have been) at risk of overexposure to lead, it is advisable to get regular blood tests and seek medical advice.

EQUIPMENT FOR ENAMELLING

You will need general items of jewellery-making equipment for the construction of pieces. Beyond that, the methods are reassuringly low-tech. A few simple hand tools and basic equipment is all that is needed to enamel. Specialist enamel tools are listed below. The most essential and expensive piece of equipment to purchase is the kiln.

Kilns

There are several types of kiln available. The main choice initially is whether to purchase a gas or an electric kiln. The choice beyond that is largely determined by what size of kiln you will want to run. The factors to consider are:

- safety features
- pyrometer/temperature gauges

- the size of your workshop, the usable space, the kiln position and set-up required
- the availability of ventilation
- the size and quantity of the work you want to make
- running costs
- maintenance factors
- the type of door/muffle (most kiln doors are designed for right-handed people. If you are left-handed, it is worth considering the door type and repositioning of handles/opening methods).

Whatever your choice, a kiln should be positioned in a safe, well-ventilated area, on a heatproof surface.

To adequately fire enamel, kilns must be able to reach temperatures of 700° to 950°C.

Gas kilns

Generally, gas kilns are available in three sizes and are ready-fitted with temperature controls and gauge. They can be fitted to the main gas supply or can be run on bottled gas. Gas kilns heat up quickly and are practical to use. The main consideration with a gas kiln is its position and its suitability for your workshop conditions, and the essential need for ventilation. Gas kilns must have a direct ventilation system. Doors are side-opening, and the running costs are based on the replacement of the gas bottle or the cost of gas supply. Over time, the floor tile will occasionally need to be replaced.

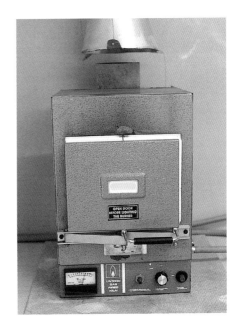

Gas kiln

Electric kilns

Electric kilns are available in a wide range of standard sizes. Small, tabletop-size kilns are popular with beginners producing small articles. It is also possible to have an electric kiln built for specific requirements. It is essential that electric kilns should be fitted with a safety device that isolates the current under fault conditions. The heating element in an electric kiln is encased in an insulating, heat-resistant material. The fitting of a pyrometer and thermostat is needed in

Electric kiln

order to regulate temperature. Running costs are dependent on the size of kiln and the level of usage. The element may need to be replaced over time.

Tools and safety equipment for enamelling
- *To grind enamel:* A good-quality, acidproof, ceramic pestle and mortar (not marble or steel).
- *To apply enamel:* Quills, paintbrushes, palette knives, enamel pots, tweezers, sgraffito tools, stencils, a set of sifters, and kitchen roll/paper for absorbing moisture.
- *For painted enamel:* A glass muller, a glass tile and fine sable brushes.
- *To fire the enamel:* Heatproof gloves are essential. Firing tongs, steel meshes, ceramic fibreboard, trivets for balancing work and mica sheets for plique à jour are also needed. Metal tweezers and/or a palette knife are needed for moving work when hot.
- *For 'stoning':* Carborundum stones/sticks, diagrit pads, emery paper, pumice, a leather stick and a glass brush.
- *For dry sifting of enamel:* Wear a dust/respirator mask (i.e. 3M code 9322).
- *For eye protection:* Wear safety glasses or UV protection goggles (the same as welders' goggles).

Equipment for applying enamel: fine mesh sifter for sieving, assorted sgraffito tools, paint brushes, quills, found items for stencilling, enamel pots and pallet

Above: Diagrit pads, carborundum sticks, emery paper and glass brush

Left: Steel meshes, trivets, ceramic fibreboard, mica, firing tongs, pallet knife and tweezers

CHAPTER TWO

ENAMEL TYPES

Enamel is a form of glass. Its constituent parts are a combination of glass flux with silica, flint, soda or potash, and borax, each element effecting the composition and fluidity of the enamel. The addition of metal oxides gives the substance its colours. Other compounds are notably present in some enamel: lead, for example, is used in clear fluxes and a number of colours for brilliance, and tin is added to enamel to give it its opaque properties.

The different types of enamel are as follows:

- **Opaque enamels** are totally solid in colour. They can be used over silver and gold but are more typically used over copper.
- **Opalescent enamels** have a beautiful, milky, iridescent quality. There is a more limited colour range in opalescent enamels. They are best fired over an engraved surface to catch the light through the metal surface, allowing the sheen of the colour to show through. Firing of opalescent colours can be tricky, and will require practice. The first firing should be high, whilst the second firing requires a lower rate of heat to reduce the finish to its required opalescence.
- **Transparent colours** let light through to reveal the metal surface. They also need to be fired over engraved or textured surfaces. Transparent colours look best when washed thoroughly and ground coarsely. They are mostly used over silver and gold, as these metals have good reflective qualities.
- **Painted enamel** is very finely ground, powdered enamel oxide from which a wide range of effects can be produced. Painted enamels can be used over opaque, opalescent or transparent enamels. When mixed, the enamel is applied with a fine brush over a previously enamelled base coat. Images are built up in layers over several firings. Colours can be purchased as underglaze or overglaze colours. Underglaze colours need an additional layer of clear flux to finish and protect the image.
- **Liquid enamel** is finely ground enamel that is suspended in an aqueous

Opposite: Transparent enamel frit

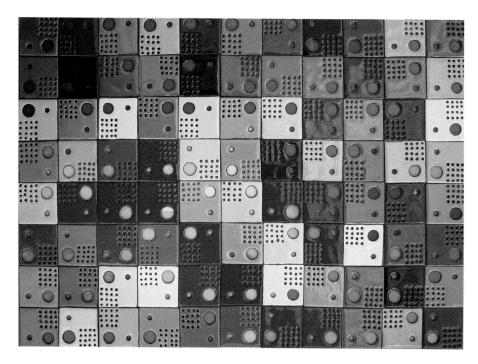

Opaque colour samples on copper by Chris Walker. Photo: Ruth Ball

solution combined with special additives. Liquid enamel can be applied by dipping, spraying, pouring or painting onto the metal surface.

Each enamel colour, in addition to its type, has a different fusing characteristic. The melting temperature of enamel can vary, as outlined below:

- Soft enamels are those that fire at a low melting range, from about 730° to 780°C.
- Medium enamels fire in the mid range of between 780° and 840°C.
- Hard enamels have the highest melting point, firing at temperatures above 840°C.

Generally, it is important to fire colours from the same firing groups together. This produces the best results. However, some interesting effects can be achieved by firing soft colours over hard, and vice versa. The colours break through one another and cause spotting or salt-and-pepper effects. Light and dark colours used together can produce effective results.

Enamels will burn out if overfired, but they may also produce alternative solutions if controlled. Certain opaque colours over copper, for example, when overfired will become transparent. Testing colour combinations, experimenting with careful observation and developing adequate control of your blending method can create alternative mixtures for a specific purpose.

Enamel flux is basically clear transparent enamel, and not a flux as in the term used for silver soldering. Flux is used for various reasons. It can be used as a base for transparent colours, or as a base for embedding *cloisonné* wires. It is used as a protective coating over painted enamel and foil, or it can be used as a colour effect. Flux reflects the whiteness of the metal when fired onto silver. Over copper, reacting with the oxide, flux can be a range of colours from yellow through to pinkish-orange and red-brown hues. Special fluxes can be used for specific requirements. A blue flux can be used, for instance, to enhance certain red transparents.

MAKING TESTS

The different ways of combining enamel are quite extensive; therefore, the only way to determine the success of colour compatibility is to make a test piece, firing all colours together and noting the rate at which different colours fire. The

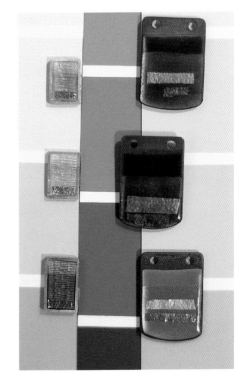

accumulated test that you create will form an essential guide for your reference. Unfortunately, enamels are not labelled as to their firing characteristics, so an element of discovery is part of the challenge.

It is useful to create a firing test for each individual colour you use. Small tests are best done on the metal you want to fire the colours onto. However, firing over copper and adding a layer of flux and gold/silver foil to the test strip is a useful and more economical method. The colours over each material will give an indication of the hue over the flux and the different metals.

The choices of enamel colour are many. It is worth noting that some

Transparent colour sample tests by
Ruth Ball

colours require specific treatment. For example, most blues and greens are generally stable colours and will fire well in most situations; however, all transparent reds and pinks, and some yellows and oranges, need to be fired over a layer of flux. Reds in particular burn out very quickly, so careful control when firing is essential. Some opaque whites will overfire rapidly and some opaque blacks prefer only two or three firings. The testing of colours is essential in learning the properties of each enamel colour and the variety of its firing possibilities.

ADDITIONAL MATERIALS

In conjunction with enamel a range of other products can be used for added embellishment.

Threads

Threads are very fine rods of enamel that can be purchased in a range of colours. Bought threads are uniform in structure and, although not often used by designer enamellers, they provide possibilities for decorative effect. Threads are placed with tweezers or a brush on a fired base of enamel, and on firing will sink into the base layer. They can be left submerged in the enamel as a semi-raised surface, or subsequent layers of enamel can be added, then stoned back to give a smooth surface revealing finely coloured lines of enamel within a solid enamel surface.

Millefiori

Millefiori are decorative glass elements that can be fused within enamel. They are made from rods of glass that have coloured sections fused within them, making decorative shapes. Millefiori require a long, high firing, as they are thick and have a

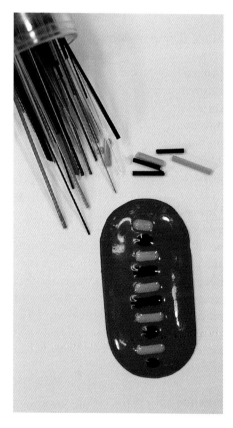

Enamel threads and test piece. Copper press form shape. Ruth Ball

greater glassy constitution than the enamel. They are pretty but are tricky to use within designed work, as they are highly decorative in their own right.

Glass beads
Tiny glass seed beads can be fused into enamel. Be very careful only to experiment with glass beads. Do not fire plastic beads, as firing plastic is not only dangerous, but toxic, and you will also make a nasty mess. Beads can be positioned on a base of enamel with Klyre fire (see p.22) or medium. On firing, the beads will fuse with the enamel. They can be used to give additional surface interest or can be stoned back for further decorative effects.

Lumps
Lumps are actually small chunks of enamel frit, which is the solid state of the enamel before grinding. When fired onto a base of enamel the lump/frit will spread out and fire into bloblike shapes within the base enamel. The thickness of the enamel and fired frit/lump must be consistent; if the pieces are too highly raised they may crack or pop off.

Lustres
Lustres are metallic or coloured compounds suspended in an oil-based medium. They give a pearly, irridescent finish to the enamel surface. They are applied to the enamel on the final firing, painted on in thin layers, and can be used for highlighting or special effects. Lustres can be thinned down with lustre essence/special thinners. Lustres should be allowed to dry fully before firing, and care should be taken when firing as fumes are released, so good ventilation is essential. Applying lustre takes a little practice, as it needs to be fired at low temperatures and will have a tendency to burn out rapidly if overfired. Conversely, it will rub off if underfired.

Fineline inks
Fineline inks are intense painting colours that are premixed in an oil-based medium. They are only

Fineline ink, overglaze black on opaque white enamel, test piece. Ruth Ball available in black and white, but offer a convenient, ready-mixed solution that can be applied with a brush or pen to add details.

Holding agents

There are different substances that are useful for the binding of enamel when firing and positioning.

- Klyre fire is a water-based, organic gum which acts as a binder for the enamel but will burn out without trace.
- Gum tragacanth is also an organic, water-based gum.
- Medium is organic aromatic oil used in the mixing of painted enamel (e.g. pine oil or lavender oil). The oil has to be evaporated out before the work is fired, otherwise it will affect the surface of the image. Medium gives off fumes, particularly on heating, so use it in a well-ventilated area.

Decals

It is possible to use special, ceramic-based transfers with enamel. The transfer, commonly known as 'decal', is the same as those used in the ceramic industry. The system for application to the enamel is identical. Basically, the image, which is printed in pigment onto specialist paper, is dampened. The image is then floated onto the enamel surface. The paper is soaked off and removed. The piece is then dried and fired. Designs can be bought commercially, or bespoke designs can be commissioned via specialist companies. Instructions for use can be obtained from the suppliers.

Scalex/ball clay

Scalex can be painted over metal to act as an oxide inhibitor. It is also useful for painting on the reverse of a piece when counter enamel may stick to meshes. Scalex is a sliplike substance. It should be dried off if it is used in the kiln. It is only suitable for the back of work when the back section is not on view.

ENAMEL PREPARATION

Enamel can be bought in lump or powdered form. Lump, also called frit, is preferred for longevity. It does not deteriorate over time. However, for convenience powdered enamel is quite adequate, and if stored correctly will last well.

There are three main ways of using enamel: dry sifting with sieves; wet laying with quills/brushes; and painting techniques using finely ground enamel oxides.

- Sifting allows the enamel to be graded dry; with this method no washing of the enamel is needed.
- When employing wet-laying techniques, or if using transparent colours, the washing and grinding of colour is important. Washing is done, not particularly to remove dirt, but to wash out the fine silt formed when grinding.
- Painted enamel needs to be ground with oil-based medium, or in some cases with distilled water.

Sifting

Sifting is the term used for applying dry enamel to the metal with sieves. The term is also used as an expression for grading the enamel particles. Grade sifting is done to maintain a defined, regular particle size. When enamel is bought in powder form, unless otherwise stated, the mix is a general grind of particles.

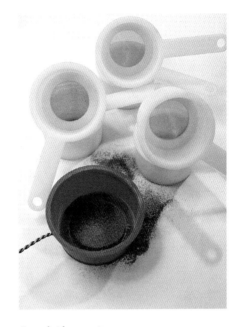

Set of sifts, or sieves

Particles of enamel are often referred to in mesh sizes. The fine meshes used for sifting are measured by the number of holes per square inch. The size of enamel therefore relates to the enamel grain size when passing through the mesh. A number of mesh sizes are used. The meshes are contained in small containers called sifts or sieves. They can be bought in individual sizes or they can be purchased as stacking sets.

The reasons for requiring different grades of enamel are various. As a general guide the following may be helpful:

- 60/80 mesh: Sieved at this grade, enamel looks like fine grains of sand or sugar. It can be used for transparent and *plique à jour* methods. If ground too finely, transparent colours can lose their clarity. For *plique à jour*, the particle size needs to be quite coarse to enable a more cohesive bond when firing across the open cell framework.
- 100/150 mesh: A common sifting size for dry applications, and suitable for general wet-laying methods and for opaque colours.
- 200/300 mesh: This grade is useful for wet-packing fine, narrow spaces. In sifting techniques finer sifts can create toned effects.
- 325/400 mesh: Described as 'fines', the enamel looks like talcum powder in

consistency. It is ground at this level for several reasons. The flux for painted enamel requires a very fine surface coating. The grains of enamel have to be very small, as otherwise they would lift the painted image they cover. Colours such as opaque white benefit from being ground finely. The enamel made with 'fines' can be mixed with water or gum and painted onto a previously fired layer of enamel to create a watercolour effect. Additionally, if you are firing pieces three-dimensionally, the enamel adheres better if the particles are finer, enabling them to cover more densely.

It is worth considering the firing variances in relation to mesh size. Smaller particles will fire more quickly than larger particles, and will also fire at lower temperatures.

Grinding

Lump (frit) enamel must be ground in order to form it into a granular powdered state. The grinding of enamel from lump is done largely to determine the particle size. The lump enamel is ground down to size using a pestle and mortar.

Grinding method

- Put a small amount of enamel lump into a ceramic mortar bowl and add a little water, just enough to cover.
- Place a kitchen towel over the pestle and mortar so that it catches any particles as the lump is being broken down.
- Hit the lump sharply several times until it breaks down into smaller sizes. Rock the pestle firmly over sections that are harder to crush, if needed.
- Remove the kitchen towel and pour a little more water over the enamel lump.
- Grind in a circular motion, working on the centre of the bowl. You should aim to grind the enamel steadily, rather than just swirl it around. A firm pressure should be maintained.
- Keep checking the enamel to observe particle size. Periodically, tip away the cloudy water to check the grains. When the enamel is coarse, the grinding sounds gritty, and when it is fine it will sound smoother and glassier. Stop when you have the viscosity you need.

Washing

Washing of the ground particles is done to remove any possible contaminants; for example, dust/impurities/residues in the enamel. It is also done to refine and wash away any very fine, overground enamel, with the aim of leaving regular particle sizes in the main body of enamel. Tap water can be used for rinsing ground enamel, but for the best effect purified/distilled water should be used. This gives the best clarity and avoids further contamination.

'Hit' the enamel to break down the frit/lump

Grind enamel using the pestle and mortar

Rinse enamel in distilled water until the water is clear, not cloudy

Enamel washed and ground to different grain sizes

Washing method

- Fill to the top of the mortar with distilled water, tap the side and allow to settle for a few seconds.
- Pour the cloudy water away; be careful not to wash the enamel away with it.
- Refill and repeat the process several times until the enamel can be seen clearly through the water.
- In the final rinses the enamel should settle rapidly and the water should be clear, with no clouding.
- Transfer the enamel to a small, watercolour dish/pallet, which should be kept covered.
- Preferably use on the same day.

Once ground the enamel should be used as soon as possible. It can be fully dried and stored in airtight containers if required. It should not be stored suspended in water for longer than a day or so, as over time enamel will deteriorate if left in contact with water.

METALS AND METAL PREPARATION

The choice of metal within jewellery enamelling is limited to copper, silver or higher carat gold alloys. Any metals alloyed with zinc or nickel are not suitable; this includes standard 9-carat gold. You should use an enamel-quality 9-carat alloy instead. Each metal has its own unique qualities when fired with enamel.

- **Copper** is economic, and useful for learning the basics. It is a good base for opaque works. If you are using copper for transparent colours, the metal does not have the same reflectivity as silver or gold. To get a result with transparent colours over copper an initial flux layer is needed as a base. Transparent colours over copper can be further improved by inlaying gold or silver foils over the flux to enhance the quality of colour.
- **Silver** fires an extensive colour range and works well with transparent, opaque and opalescent colours.
- **Gold** fuses beautifully and the colour ranges are excellent. Due to the difference in metal colour, the colours show slight variations to the effects obtained over silver.
- **Platinum** is not often used for enamelling. Its high price prevents much experimentation.
- **Other metals**, such as steel, can be enamelled, but they must be coated with liquid enamel before coloured enamels are applied. Enamel panellists commonly use steel.

The metals most suitable for enamelling are copper, silver, and higher-carat golds

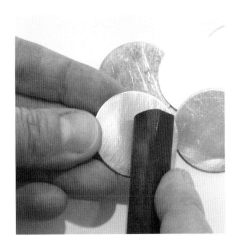

Copper is sanded with emery paper to remove surface oxide

Washing in water with a glass brush helps to remove grease deposits. Always make sure you wear gloves to protect your fingers from glass fibres in the brush

Metal preparation

The preparation of the metal surface is very important. The metal area that is to take the enamel must be free from any dirt, grease and oxide/fire stain. If any of these are present it will affect the colours, and the results will be disappointing. Even finger grease is a contaminant to enamel. You must always remember not to touch the enamel, or the areas to be enamelled, once prepared. Always enamel the work as soon as possible once it has been cleaned; alternatively, wrap it in tissue and enamel it as soon as you can.

The methods for cleaning metals vary slightly, and different pickling solutions can be used ('pickle' is a general term for the chemicals used to clean metals). The two most common solutions used are:

- Diluted sulphuric acid: A weak solution is mixed as one part acid to nine parts water, or a stronger solution can be used (one part acid to five parts water). Sulphuric acid is used for pickling copper, silver and gold. It should be mixed with care, slowly, using cold water. The acid should be added to the water, not vice versa.
- Sodium hydrogen sulphate (safety pickle): This is an effective alternative to sulphuric acid. It is purchased as a dry powder and mixed with water following the supplier's instructions. It works better when the solution is kept at a warm temperature, with effective ventilation to avoid any vapours.

Acids should always be situated in a well-ventilated area, as even vapours are harmful. All acids are corrosive, and safety instructions should always be followed fully. Remember to use plastic tweezers in pickle solutions, not metal tweezers with either steel or iron content, as these will react with the pickle.

Copper

Copper is easy to clean. It must be grease-free, particularly if you are using transparent colours. Rigorous cleaning is needed, as transparent colours will reveal irregularities in the metal surface. The annealed metal should be wet-sanded with emery paper or pumiced back to remove the oxide layer, using water with a few drops of dishwashing detergent. The piece should then be immersed in the pickle. Pickling serves to further remove the copper oxides/fire stain that are formed when the metal is heated above about 650°C. After pickling, the piece should be rinsed in water to remove any residual pickle solution. Rinsing underwater with a glass brush will ensure further cleaning/removal of grease. Dry the piece before enamelling.

Standard silver

Standard silver contains fire stain (oxide), which must be removed before enamelling. Enamel will not fire well over fire stain; it will give problems with the finish, and it will also produce muddy colours. It is better to design and construct your piece so that fire stain is prevented from forming.

It is possible to protect against fire stain forming whilst soldering parts to your piece by coating the area to be enamelled with a layer of inhibitor; for instance a soldering flux, such as auflux, FM flux, borax or Scalex. This will make the metal less prone to oxidising. If you are engraving or etching, the oxide will presumably have been removed from the surface that is to be enamelled, so general pickling should be an adequate cleaning method.

If fire stain is a problem, it is possible, with controlled heating and immersion in pickle, to raise a layer of fine silver to the surface of standard silver and eliminate the fire stain. The silver should be heated carefully to the point when the light-grey fire stain is formed. The silver should then be immersed in pickle until clean, then removed and brushed with a brass/glass brush under running water. The process should be repeated until the silver is white in appearance. This helps remove the copper oxide present in the silver and leaves a layer of fine silver on the surface of the metal. Care must be given to any soldered elements of your piece not to expose them to excessive heating, as they will burn out and become brittle. You should protect yourself against any potential splashes from the pickle solution and follow all safety instructions. This is a tricky procedure, which will require some practice. But it is not a foolproof method, and some residual oxide may remain. Transparent colours in particular will be effected by small amounts of oxide, resulting in dull patches or spotting in the surface.

If needed, the fire stain can be removed by immersion in nitric acid. General safety pickle or sulphuric acid will remove light surface oxide, but deeper oxidation can be removed via repeated dipping of the piece in nitric acid. However, using nitric acid is a dangerous hazard and is not really recommended. It is essential to stress that all health and safety guidelines should be followed for the correct handling of any acid, particularly nitric. It is extremely corrosive, and the vapours, which are constantly given off, should never be inhaled. If you have to use it, only ever do so in a controlled, well-ventilated, specialist area under supervision, wearing full safety clothing. Using nitric-acid cleaning as a process should be avoided if possible.

Cleaning method A
- Mix a strong, but diluted solution of nitric acid (one part water to one part acid), mixing the solution with cold water by adding acid to water. Use the solution at room temperature.
- Dip the piece briefly (a few seconds) into the acid solution. It will turn dark grey.
- Remove the piece and rinse with a glass brush under running water.
- Repeat the process until the grey fire stain is gone and the silver looks whitish.
- Rinse thoroughly and neutralise in baking soda if needed.

Left top: Placing silver into nitric acid. Left middle: In nitric acid the silver turns dark grey. Left bottom: Immersion in nitric removes the oxide (fire stain) and the silver appears white in colour. Right: Rinsing in water with a glass brush removes residue.

Cleaning method B

Method B involves raising the temperature of the nitric acid very slightly to hasten its action. This is potentially very dangerous and should be done with extreme care. When overactivated, nitric acid will produce a very nasty brown vapour called nitric oxide. It is severely poisonous and must not be inhaled.

- Place the piece in a shallow dish and cover with a small amount of nitric acid.
- Add a couple of drops of hot (but not boiling) water. The piece will turn black/ dark grey.
- Remove immediately from the acid. Rinse the piece in running water and glass-brush the oxide layer.
- Place the piece in acid again, briefly. The silver should turn white again.
- Remove the piece again, immediately. Then rinse in running water and glass brush. The piece should be bright, white in colour and clear of oxide.
- If the process is slow to work, it is possible to keep dipping in acid and rinsing until the oxide is removed.
- The piece should finally be neutralised in baking soda and rinsed under running water with a glass brush.

Note that, with either method, if the piece has too much contact with nitric acid there is also the danger of etching it; also the acid may weaken solder joints.

Fine silver

Fine silver does not contain fire stain, as it does not have the copper alloy content. It is a very soft metal, so the design of any enamel section should be considered in terms of wear. The cleaning method is the same as for copper, i.e. general degreasing with emery paper or pumice, immersion in safety pickle, followed by rinsing and washing with a glass brush to ensure grease-free surfaces.

Gold

The cleaning method for gold is the same as for fine silver and copper. The piece should be degreased, then immersed in pickle (either safety pickle or sulphuric acid solution). On removal from pickle the piece should be glass-brushed under running water to clean it further. For a quicker action, gold can be immersed in the pickle hot, but great care should be taken to guard against splashing, as pickles are corrosive and can cause injury to eyes and skin (wear goggles and full safety clothing).

Pickle and enamel

It is advisable to plan the final finish and polishing of an enamelled piece. In general, enamel colours are acid-resistant, but some colours will react in pickle, affecting the surface of the enamel. The surface, if affected, will become watermarked, porous or pitted. It is best to minimise the time in the pickle for the final cleaning of metal parts. Sensitive colours can be painted with colourless nail varnish or lacquer for protection in the pickle. The varnish should be removed before final polishing.

HEALTH AND SAFETY WITH ACID CHECKLIST

- Acid should only ever be used in a specialist fume cupboard with full ventilation.
- Only ever add acid to water, never water to acid.
- Only mix and store acid in suitable containers (glass or plastic) and always label them carefully and appropriately.
- All safety clothing should be worn: goggles, mask, safety gauntlets, safety apron, solid footwear, etc.
- Baking soda (sodium bicarbonate) should be kept to hand to neutralise any accidental spillages.
- Acid should always be disposed of safely, in accordance with local health authority guidelines.
- Seek immediate medical help in the event of injury or inhalation.

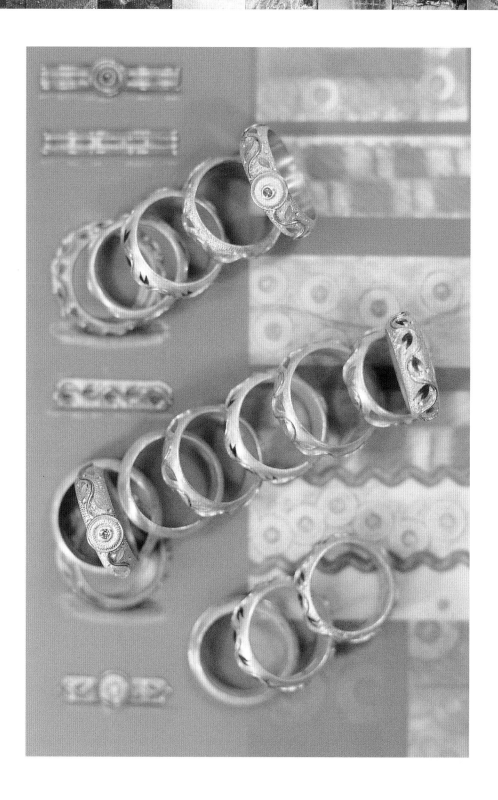

CHAPTER THREE

DESIGNING FOR ENAMEL

CONSTRUCTION METHODS

Designing for enamel involves basic planning and an awareness of suitable construction methods. There are a few common techniques that lend themselves to be used in enamelled jewellery forms. Often a series of techniques can be used to build the desired construction.

- **Engraving, etching or die-stamping** will provide the cut recesses in which the enamel can be placed. Specific and very precise designs can be produced to graphic effect.
- **Setting** can be employed on a practical or decorative level to incorporate sections of enamel into a design. Enamelling a piece then setting it separately is an excellent way of avoiding any soldered component. There are many options for setting. The type of setting employed should combine to match the work it supports.
- **Chasing and** *repoussé* techniques enable the shaping of more three-dimensional forms, giving greater interest to the overall form of a piece. *Repoussé* is a technique that enables you to create a relief design by hammering the reverse side of the metal to form a shape. In this process the piece of annealed metal is worked from a flat sheet, supported by pitch, a tar-like substance. The supporting pitch means that the metal can be pushed out with punches whilst hammering, without being damaged. Chasing is the process whereby the metal shape formed by pushing the shape out is then filled with pitch and hammered from the other side, with punches, to create more complex shapes.
- **Press-formed shapes**, typically cushioned in format, lend themselves well to enamel. The added advantage of this method is that repeated shapes can be made very easily and at low cost.
- **Castings** can be enamelled but will often be problematic. The casting has to be of a very high quality and must not be porous.

Design illustration and enamelled silver rings with
18-carat gold detail by Ruth Ball

Enamelled copper brooch section with bespoke silver setting and amber stone.
Ruth Ball

The assembly of pieces can be achieved via different methods. Soldering, riveting or screw-fitting provide adequate methods of fixing the various fittings. There are points to consider with each method:

- **Solder** cannot be used near any enamel parts, as it will discolour the enamel and may cause it to chip off. Soldered pieces can be used if they are not adjacent to enamel parts. The solder must be hard-fusing or enamel-quality solder that will stand up to repeated firings in the kiln. Specific hard-enamel solder can be used, but most enamellers tend to use standard hard solder. Eutectic and 'IT' solder for silver as well as medium 18-carat gold solders are also useful.
- **Riveting** is a useful method of joining two sections together without soldering. The position of the rivet in the design has to be considered. Rivets must be situated so that they do not crack the enamel. A common, simple solution to joining two parts is to use tube rivets. These rivets, soldered to the back of a piece, reduce the pressure when the enamel section is assembled. The tube is splayed out gently, forming a secure hold over the two sections. The rivet can be countersunk and hidden, or decorated to combine with the piece's overall design.
- **Screw-fitting** is an ideal method for putting complex shapes together. No pressure is placed on the enamel areas, and the fixings are permanently secure whilst enabling the piece to be dismantled in the event of future repair work. Sections can be constructed to form larger pieces or more complex forms.

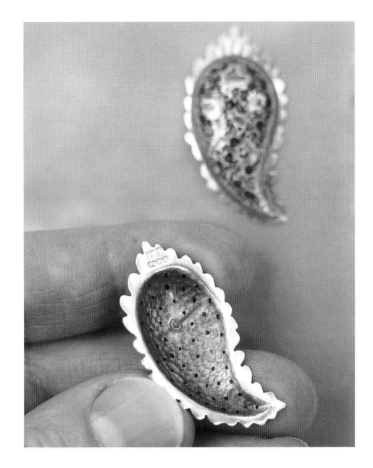

*Paisley earrings
by Ruth Ball.
Transparent pink
counter-enamel
over silver.
Photo: Ruth Ball*

Counter-enamel

An important factor in the creation of enamel pieces is that the metal and the enamel expand and contract at different rates. It is therefore essential to understand the basic processes needed to prevent the metal warping.

Counter-enamel is applied to balance out this characteristic. A layer of enamel is fired to the back of a piece. The enamel that is used should be similar in fusibility and thickness to the layers applied to the front of the piece. It acts to strengthen the piece and prevents warping of the metal. Applying enamel to the front and back of the piece means the expansions involved are evened out. In the case of bowls or pieces that are to have both sides of the article showing, counter-enamel of a complementary colour can be used to enhance the piece's overall effect.

The metal thickness determines the need for counter-enamel. Other elements to consider for all enamel designs are the thickness of enamel glaze required and, importantly, the size and shape of the article. Pieces that are curved or domed are less prone to warping, because the metal is structurally stable and stronger when formed, and thus thinner metal sections can be permitted. Smaller pieces are less likely to warp than larger pieces. Certain shapes will warp more than others. For example, rounded, curved shapes perform better than triangular, flat shapes. With a rounded shape the surface is even, but with flat triangular shapes, the points of the triangle are thinner in surface area and therefore more prone to bending.

- Any metal below 1.0 mm in thickness, either flat or domed, should be counter-enamelled. Curved or domed metal will have fewer tendencies to warp.
- Metal 1-1.3 mm in thickness can be enamelled without counter-enamel if it is domed, but needs counter-enamel if it is flat.
- With metal above 1.3 mm in thickness counter-enamel is not needed. Pieces can be flat in construction and will not have the same tendency to warp because of the greater thickness of metal. Thicker metal sections are more suited to champlevé techniques, where metal has to be carved away to form the recesses for enamel.

It should be noted that this guide refers to silver and copper. The cohesion rates for gold are different, and thinner sections of gold may be enamelled without counter-enamel.

FIRING

Enamel fuses very quickly. The exact length of firing time will be different for each piece, although firing is generally between 30 and 90 seconds. All enamel must be fully dry when inserted into the kiln. Moisture from wet-packing techniques, applications of gum or painted medium must be dried off, either by briefly holding the piece in front of the open door/muffle of the kiln or by leaving it to dry in a dust-free area of the workshop.

On fusing with the metal, enamel goes through several changes in state and appearance (see image opposite). It is possible to estimate the approximate temperature of the kiln by viewing its internal colour. These figures are approximate but offer a rough guide.

	°C	°F
Dull cherry red	700+	1300+
Cherry red	760+	1400+
Orange-red	850+	1550+
Orange-yellow	900+	1600+
Yellow-white	950+	1650+

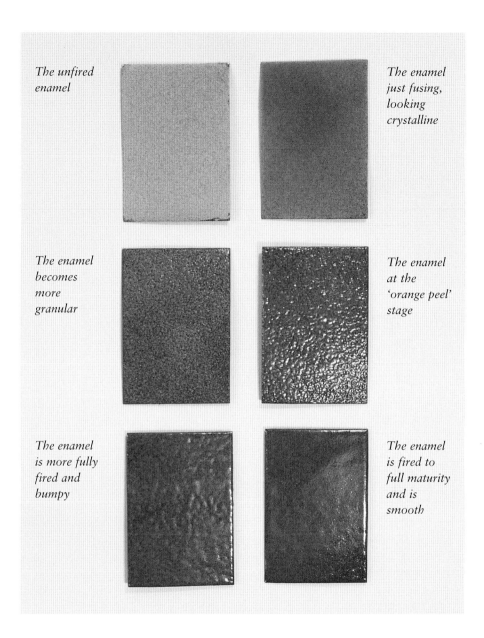

The unfired enamel

The enamel just fusing, looking crystalline

The enamel becomes more granular

The enamel at the 'orange peel' stage

The enamel is more fully fired and bumpy

The enamel is fired to full maturity and is smooth

Generally, when firing enamel, a high temperature and a short, rapid firing is best. However, control of the temperature can be very important in the various techniques. Low-firing and high-firing methods can be varied and combined for differing effects.

An essential part of the design process is planning how to support the piece when it is fired. The article that is being fired needs to be able to sit securely on a mesh, or balance steadily on a trivet. It is occasionally necessary to custom-make a supporting device for this work. Three-dimensional pieces pose the most challenges.

Ceramic fibreboard is a useful firing support. It is highly heat-reflective and will withstand temperatures of up to 1260°C. It can be useful in preventing warping when firing flat sections, and can be customised to hold individual items on firing. It can be cut and shaped with a craft knife, and drilled by hand, although great care should be taken with dust control, as fibreboard will be powdery when cut and the internal fibres should not be inhaled (work in a ventilated area and wear a dust mask).

Firing on a mesh

A variety of trivets are useful for shaped articles. Meshes can be added to with mesh wire and shaped to aid the support of a three-dimensional piece or work that needs to hang. Always balance and check the suitability of support before firing.

FINISHES

A range of surfaces can be achieved through the control of different processes. The enamel surface is typically glossy, but it can be treated to become matt, satin or granular in texture. Likewise the surrounding metal may be designed as a highly polished, textured or matted element.

To matt the enamel surface there are two methods. Stoning back the enamel surface by hand, with carborundum or diagrit pads, reveals a stony matt texture. Immersing your piece in a chemical solution called 'matting salts' will give a smooth matt surface.

To create a granular texture, the final layer of enamel or an overlay of clear flux can be underfired in the final firing, leaving an interesting crystalline surface. Alternatively, added elements can be fired with or into the enamel. For example, including extra silica in the enamel gives a granite-like appearance. Firing tiny glass seed beads in the final firing adds a texture and surface interest.

Rings: Chris Walker. Example of matted granular surface with silica. Photo: Chris Walker

Surrounding metal surfaces can be machine-polished but are best polished by hand, especially if the enamel surface has been treated with a matt or alternative finish, as the compounds for polishing may affect the enamel. Hand polishing gives better control of the piece so that the enamel sections are not damaged.

    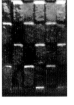 

Stoned matt   *Underfired flux over black*   *Underfired flux over gloss black*   *Glass seed beads over black*   *Raised gloss*   *Underfired black*

Six black enamel sample finishes. *Photographs: Andra Nelki*

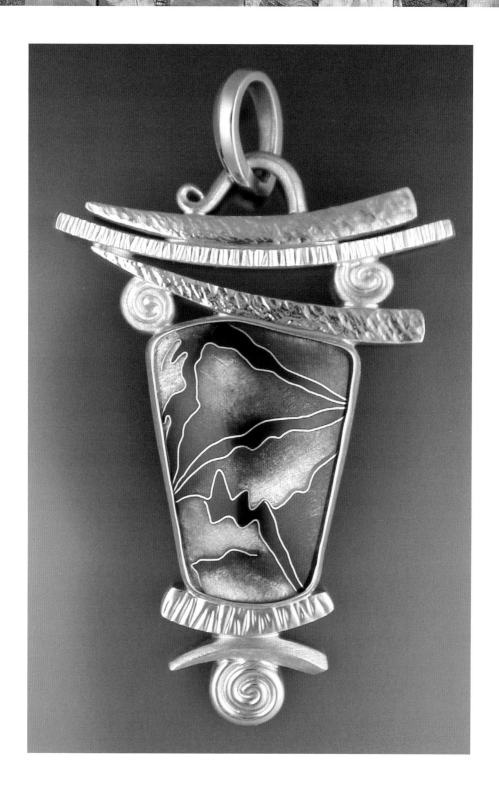

CHAPTER FOUR

CLOISONNÉ

Cloisonné is thought to be the oldest enamel technique. The fusing of fine wires to a base coat of enamel creates the *cloisonné* method. The design is built up by placing the various enamel colours into the cells that are formed by the wires.

WIRES FOR CLOISONNÉ

Cloisonné wires can be fashioned from copper, silver or gold. Traditionally, wires are rectangular, although round wires can also be used. It is equally possible to forge, file and shape irregular sections of wire to fuse into the enamel for more free-form/expressive effects. The wires for all methods are very fine. It is possible to use different diameters of round wire. It is worth making samples to explore the quality and thickness of line and the different enamel depth that is achieved.

Round wire is easier to shape and stays in place more readily. The depth achieved using round wire will depend on the diameter of wire used. Extremely fine round wire of 0.1 mm diameter is suitable only as a surface effect, whereas 0.3 mm is a good general size to work with. Round wire of 0.5 mm, possibly the thickest round diameter that is of general use, will lend greater depth to transparent colours.

Rectangular wires are generally 0.2 mm or 0.3 mm thick and around 1.5 mm deep, although there are several variations available. Rectangular wires allow for greater thickness of enamel. Rectangular wire methods can be used for a variety of effects. Problems with positioning and balance can easily be overcome via a combination of methods. Using a gum/holding agent to position the wires is beneficial, and cutting off small tabs into the rectangular strip provides stable anchors within the design, helping the wire to stand in place whilst firing.

All *cloisonné* wires should be annealed and cleaned before they are shaped and placed onto the enamel surface. Fine silver or 18-carat or 24-carat gold round wire is normally used, as the higher-carat metals require little cleaning once annealed.

Facets of Universal Colour. *Pendant by Sharon Scalise.*
Enamel, silver and gold. Photo: Alexa Smarsh

STAGES OF CLOISONNÉ CONSTRUCTION

The *cloisonné* wire used in the picture below is rectangular, but for the main set of images round, fine silver wire, 0.3 mm in diameter, was used. The wire was annealed and cleaned before being shaped and placed onto the enamel surface.

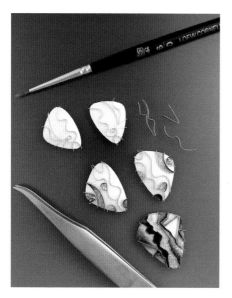

Preparation

The metal shapes were press-formed from a sheet of 0.4 mm fine silver to create a cushioned dome shape. The shapes were designed so that they could be enamelled and then set into a bezel. Once pressed out, the two matching shapes were cut to shape and cleaned in preparation for enamelling.

Left: Stages of cloisonné *construction, sections for enamel brooch by Sharon Scalise. Fashioned using rectangular fine gold* cloisonné *wires. Photo: Alex Smarsh*

Below: Fine silver press-formed shapes and formers

Applying the counter-enamel

Counter-enamel in the form of clear flux can be applied to the back of the shapes. If you grind your enamel very finely you can fire the front and back in one firing. Gum is not necessarily essential, but, to help the counter enamel remain on the back of the piece when firing, it is possible to apply a thin coating of Klyre fire to the metal surface before applying the enamel. You can then enamel the topcoat at the same time, firing with the front of the piece uppermost. If any enamel drops from the back of the piece, repeat the metal cleaning, reapply the enamel and then fire.

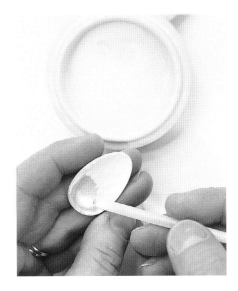

Applying the counter-enamel

Placing the wires

A layer of clear enamel flux is applied and fired. In *cloisonné* enamel, the first layer of enamel serves as a base onto which the wires are fused. Typically, a base layer is clear flux. The flux provides a neutral layer for the subsequent enamel colours.

The wires are cut to length and shaped with pliers. They are positioned carefully with a fine brush. If needed, Klyre fire can be used to keep them in place whilst firing. The wires are fired in the kiln to fix them into place, fusing them into the surface of the flux. Care must be taken not to overfire, as the wires will sink in too much and become too low down in the enamel layer.

If you use a copper base and silver wires, any overfiring will cause the silver wires to sink to the level of the copper, which results in an eutectic reaction between the metals. The metals will bond and alloy, and the piece will become unworkable.

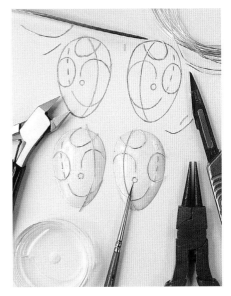

Shaping and placing the wires

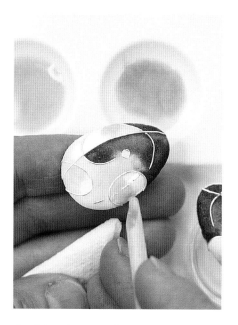

Applying the enamel

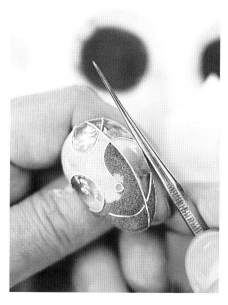

Tapping the side to even out the surface

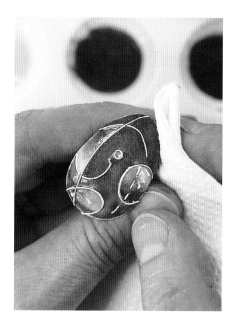

Drying moisture from the enamel with a tissue

Applying the first layer of colour

Colours are ground and washed, then applied in a thin layer covering the required areas of the design. A quill or fine brush is used to apply the enamel. Once the area is covered, the piece is tapped gently to remove any trapped air, dried with a tissue to remove moisture, and then fired in the kiln.

Applying more layers

As with most techniques, another two or three layers are applied and fired until the enamel is flush with the top level of the wires. It is necessary to build up the enamel in thin, even layers, firing each layer separately. In the wet-packing technique, each application is dried with absorbent tissue before being fired in the kiln.

The repeated fired layers build up the depth of colour and avoid any problems caused by too thick a layer being fired. If the enamel is applied too thickly, it characteristically 'balls up' or can cause air pockets, resulting in holes or chipping.

Stoning back

Once the fired enamel has reached the top of the wires it is stoned back with carborundum stone or diagrit to ensure that the piece is uniform and the enamel surface is flush with the embedded wires. The stone is used with water to grind back the surface. Using water helps prevent particles of stone becoming trapped in the enamel. The piece is also rinsed under

Stoning back the enamel surface to the level of the wires

running water with a glass brush to further clean and remove any residue before it is fired again to reglaze the enamel.

Finishing

A separate setting for the enamel is an ideal way of overcoming problems with finishing, and creates many design possibilities. Setting a piece has many advantages. The key benefit is that, once the enamel has been fired, there are no fittings or soldered parts to worry about. All metal parts can be finalised separately and assembled in a few simple steps.

Bezel-setting strip is available in standard sizes and can be purchased from metal suppliers. Alternatively, you can cut your own diameter from thin sheet to the size you require. Fine silver or higher-carat gold/fine gold is recommended for setting enamel. These metals are softer to push over when setting and will cause less stress on the enamel. Before you start, work out the depth of setting you will need. Check the depth of bezel strip you require (about 3 mm high is suitable for shallow work and something in excess of 5 mm high is better for deeper-set pieces).

To make a basic bezel setting

Cut a strip of bezel wire the same outside diameter as the enamel. Bend the wire to the shape required and solder the ends together. Check the fit, and shape the soldered wire around the enamel form.

- Cut out a base the same shape as the enamel, file it to the shape required and solder the shaped wire around the edge.
  Alternatively, solder the strip onto the base plate. The remaining rim can either be used decoratively within the design or cut away.
- Place the enamel into the setting, checking the fit. Make any alterations.
- Pickle and clean the setting then solder any fittings into position.
- Once you are happy with the fit, and have completed any finishing to the piece, with care set the enamel. The fine bezel wire should be pushed over at intervals with a bezel pusher. Start with a gentle action, first at a 12 o'clock position

Final setting with a bezel pusher tool

then 6 o'clock, then 3 o'clock and then 9 o'clock, thus enabling an even tension. Continue by pushing over in between each interval, smoothing out the bezel wire and blending it gently into the edge of the piece.

- Use a burnishing tool to give a final finish to the edge. The burnishing tool will further smooth the surface of the line and provide a polish to the edge.

Setting has to be done very cautiously, as there is the potential for putting too much pressure on the enamel and causing it to crack. Go slowly and place firm but gentle pressure on the tools, without forcing the metal.

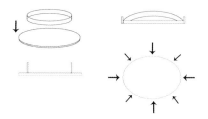

The bezel strip is soldered to shape. It is then soldered to a flat base and trimmed or otherwise made to fit the internal rim. The enamel is placed into the setting and the bezel rim is pushed gently over at intervals.

CLOISONNÉ SHOWCASE

Cloisonné is used in many ways, forming pattern or enabling illustrative or expressive effects. Noticeably, the wire creates lines that have a fluid, hand-drawn quality, allowing the colours in the piece to integrate.

Commemorative necklace by Alexandra Raphael, 2002. Silver and gold cloisonné, *pink tourmaline and lapis beads. 6.5 × 5 cm (2½ × 2 in.) and 51 cm (20 in.) long.*
Photo: John Knill

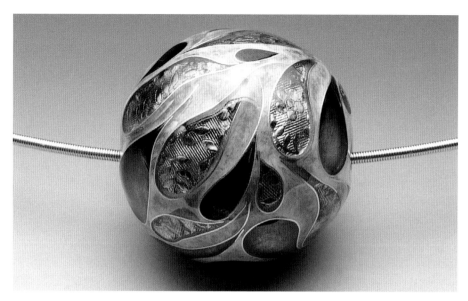

Pendant *by Erica Druin, 2004. 24-carat gold, fine silver and enamel. 3 cm (1¼ in.) diameter. Won the Niche Award for Metals: Enamel Category.*
Photo: Richard Goodbody

Layered three-dimensional brooch *by Jeanne Werge Hartley, 2002. Enamel, hardenable silver, high-carat golds and precious-metal clay. 7 × 5 cm (2¾ × 2 in.).*
Photo: Jeanne Werge Hartley

Untitled. 1999 goblet/wedding cup by Marilyn Druin. Fine silver, with 18-carat and 24-carat gold wire and foils, 5.2 cm (2 in.) diameter x 14 cm (5½ in.) height.
Photo: Mel Druin

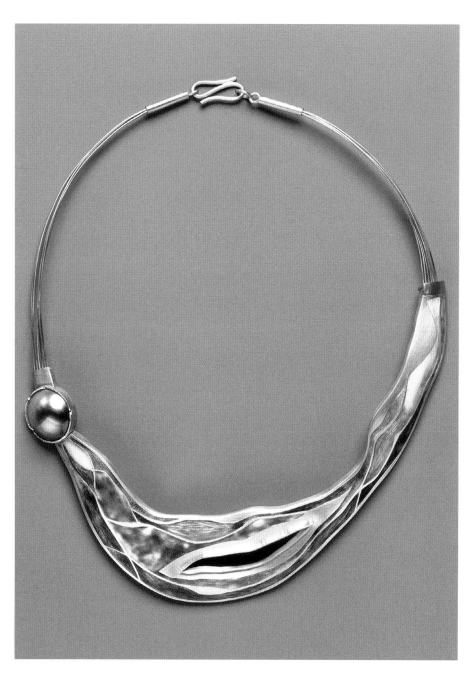

Necklace *by Sarah Letts. Enamel on silver, 18ct gold and pearl.*
Enamel section 14 x 3 cm (5½ x 1 in.). Photo: Rodney Forte

CHAPTER FIVE

CHAMPLEVÉ

The technique of *champlevé* requires the surface of the metal to be cut away to form recesses into which enamel is placed. Engraving is the most formal method used. Other methods capable of forming recessed cells are: etching, die-stamping, some *repoussè* methods and good-quality casting.

There are developments of the *champlevé* technique which make enhanced use of the metal surface, namely *basse taille*, and a method that is referred to as *guilloche*.

- *Basse taille* involves the additional engraving of pattern or image to different depths, thus enabling the metal surface to reflect through transparent enamel.
- *Guilloch* is the technical term used for the elaborate interwoven patterns that are cut in the machine process of engine turning. The brilliance and the cutting of the metal creates a luminous effect that captures the light through the transparent enamel.

ENGRAVING

Engraving is a skill that requires practice. It can be used as a technique in its own right for decorative effect. Silver and gold are the preferred metals for engraving techniques, as they are softer to carve away.

There are a number of health and safety precautions to take into account when engraving:

- Ensuring a comfortable working position saves any strain from the repetitive actions of cutting or from sitting for long periods. Always set up your working area so that you are are sitting with a straight back at a correct working height.
- It is advisable to take regular breaks from work for short periods to maintain an effective concentration level.
- Good lighting is also important when engraving, as poor lighting can strain the eyes. If needed, magnifying glasses/lenses should also be worn.

- Safety glasses/a face visor should be worn when engraving, when grinding the engraving tools to size, and also when fitting the engraver to its handle. This is to avoid any cut particles entering the eye if they flick up by accident.
- The engraver must be clamped securely when grinding to shape and size.
- Always position fingers correctly. Never have them in line with the tool when cutting. If you slip you risk cutting yourself badly. Always cut away from yourself.
- Sharpen tools regularly, and when working avoid slipping and poor cutting. Engraving tools should be sharpened to a 45-degree angle for efficient cutting.

Engraving tools

There are four basic engraving tools needed to cut away sections for enamel: a half-round, a narrow flat, a wide flat and a spitsticker.

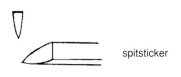

round

wide flat

narrow flat

spitsticker

- The half-round marks out the areas to be carved and sets the depth.
- The flats take away the surface needed.
- The spitsticker trims the walls of the cells on the final cutting of areas to be enamelled.

Engravers are bought without the handles fitted. They need to be sized, mounted, shaped and sharpened. This enables you to set them up to your own requirements. In the preparation of the tool it is important to grind away the top face of the engraver. This is done to create a smaller cutting face, enabling the regular sharpening of the tool to be made easier.

The four types of engraving tools needed to cut for champlevé *enamel*

Engravers are tempered to a high degree of hardness, and it is important in the grinding process not to allow the metal to become too hot. Regular cooling in water is essential. It is better to grind in short intervals so as not to build up heat in the tool. If the point is inadvertently annealed it will become too soft to work or become brittle.

The length of the shaft should also be ground away at the handle end so that the tool is the correct length for your individual grip. As a general guide the tool

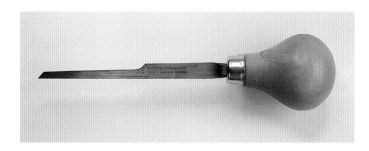

The engraver ground to shape and fitted with a wooden handle

should be comfortable to hold. The engraver should be sized so that when mounted with the handle, the engraver tip extends 0.5 to 0.75 in. (13 to 20 mm) beyond the thumb when held in the cutting position. Your index finger should rest along the top face of the engraver. The other fingers stabilise the motion and your thumb should act as an anchor to support and guide the work as it is cut. To remove surplus length from the tool, again taking care not to overheat the engraver, grind a section back to the required point at the handle end of the engraver. This is called the tang. The tang should then be ground to a pointed shape ready to fit into the wooden handle.

To fit the engraver handle, secure the shaft in a bench vice. The handle is positioned and aligned to the tool. Then it is hit with a hammer to secure the handle down onto the engraver shaft. Once the engraver is set up, it is important to emphasise that, when engraving, tools need to be kept sharp. Engravers should be sharpened to a 45° angle on a lightly oiled carborundum or Arkansas stone. Engravers will need regular sharpening as a piece is engraved. Sharpening can take some practice. The tool is moved evenly forwards and backwards up and down the stone, held firmly and with care taken not to rock the tip. Alternatively the engraver can be rubbed in a small circular motion on the stone.

It is equally important to get the correct angle for cutting. If the angle is too high or too low the cutting will be laboured. Cutting with the engraver should feel smooth. The surface of the metal is scraped away rather than gouged out. If the cutting is difficult, it normally means that the tool is not sharp or it hasn't been sharpened at the correct angle.

It is better to engrave metal that has been annealed. The cutting angle in relation to the surface being cut should be around 10 to 15° to the plane of the piece.

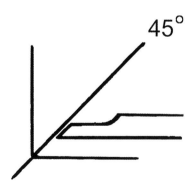

Engravers are kept sharp to a 45° angle

STAGES OF THE CHAMPLEVÉ TECHNIQUE

Marking out a design

For the design shown below, silver sheet 1.5 mm thick was used. At this thickness the metal does not need counter enamel and is thick enough not to warp. The advantage of this is that any fittings can be soldered directly to the back of the piece. This is done before marking out. Enamel pieces are fired in the kiln several times, so always solder with hard or enamel solder to ensure well-bonded joints.

The metal is marked out to create a clear image to follow. First the metal is painted with white acrylic ink, which is left to dry. When the ink is dry the design is traced onto the metal with a pencil, using carbon paper or tracing paper. The pencil line is then scribed over more accurately with a metal point. The ink is washed off once the piece has been engraved.

Engraving the cells

Once the design has been set out, the areas are engraved. The design is started with a half-round engraver, which is used to cut and mark out the design. Then the flat engravers, the wide or the narrow depending on the design, are used to carve away the recessed sections required. Cutting is done in different directions across the surface so as to maintain an even layer of cutting.

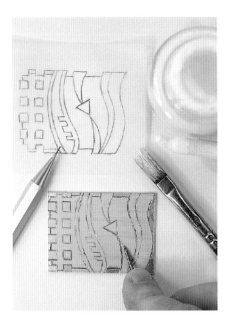

The half-round cuts the depth for the second time, then the cuts are repeated with the flat engravers down to the level required, which is normally to a depth of 0.2 or 0.3 mm depending on the design requirements. Engraving is done in stages to enable control of the surface as per the design.

The finishing cuts are made to outline the side walls of the piece using the split stick engraver. This sharpens up the design and gives it definition. Once the design is cut, each area is called a cell; typically, each cell will carry a separate colour.

Marking out the metal

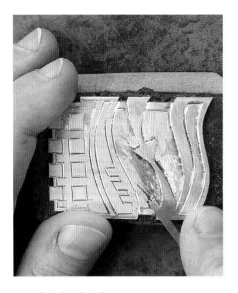

The first levels of cutting

Final cutting revealing the engraved pattern

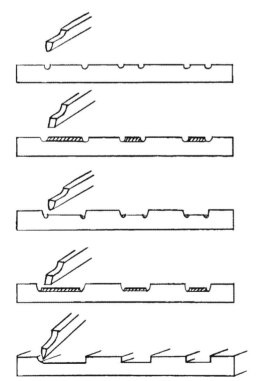

The stages of cutting:

The depth is set by carving around the outline with the half-round engraver

The areas are then cut away using the flat engravers

The depth is set again, outlining with the half-round engraver

Cutting is repeated once more with the flat engravers, keeping the surface layer even

Final cutting is made with the split stick to trim the side walls

Holding devices

For engraving, a variety of supports can be used. Sometimes work can be supported by hand, but it is often difficult to hold a piece whilst cutting. Commonly, work is fixed into an engraver's vice, or alternatively work can be supported with setter's wax on a small wooden block, which is then rested on a sandbag.

Fixing method using setter's wax

To fix the setter's wax to the block, you must heat it slowly and with care over a soft yellow flame. A number of health and safety procedures must be followed with this technique:

Engraver's vice

- Care must be taken with the wax. Protect against burns by wearing heat-resistant safety gloves.
- Never overheat the wax. Wax will bubble up quickly if overheated and will ignite.
- Hold the work, the wax and the waxed block with metal tweezers.

The wax should be smeared onto the wood so it covers the wood surface. When the surface is covered, heat the wax over the block very gently, until it is soft. While the wax is in this warm state, turn the block over and place it against a cold metal block, pressing gently to flatten the wax surface. The next stage is to heat the metal very gently. This is again done over a yellow flame, heating just enough to allow the piece to melt into the wax to fix. Place the piece over the wax and press gently to position, either with tweezers or with a metal block. The metal will sink gently into the wax and once cooled will be ready to hold.

Once the piece has been engraved, in order to remove it from the wax you can either prise the piece off the wax with a palette knife or heat carefully to soften the wax again. However, do take care not to raise the metal temperature to fire stain. Any surplus wax stuck to the back can be removed with paint stripper/white spirit before pickling.

Filling the cells

It is important to have both the metal and the enamel as clean and free from impurities as possible. Once the piece has been fully engraved the metal is cleaned to remove any oxides and grease. The enamel is ground with a pestle and mortar into a wet paste of evenly sized particles, and then washed thoroughly in distilled water.

Traditionally, the enamel is placed into the engraved recesses with a goose quill, although if preferred a fine paintbrush can be used. The quill carries the enamel well and can be cut to a variety of shapes for different cuts of recess, i.e. fine points for small cells, wider broad quills for larger cells.

As with all the techniques, the enamel is applied in stages, each section being filled in turn. Once the enamel has filled all the cells, the piece

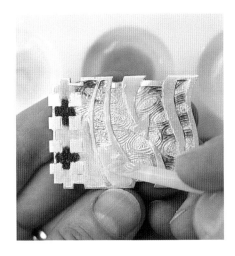

Filling the cells

is lightly tapped to expel any trapped air and then dried fully to remove all the moisture. It is then fired in the kiln. The enamel has to be applied in thin layers.

Adding foil

Before the final layer of colour, gold (or silver) foils can be applied using a fine brush and a little water to highlight certain areas. Once the foil has been laid down into position, it is then fired in the kiln. The layers of enamel that are subsequently applied trap the foil, giving it protection and lending additional extra interest to the enamel surface, either decoratively or as part of the colour range of the design. If you add a coloured transparent over the foil it will reflect the colour through its surface. If you require the foil to stay gold in colour, use a clear flux as the overlay.

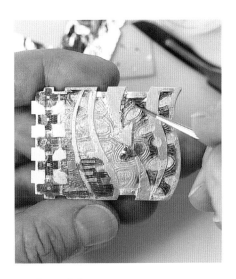

Applying foil

Stoning back

Once enough enamel has been fired to slightly overfill the cells, the surface is ground down with a carborundum stone or diagrit, so that the enamel is flush with the surface of the metal. This method is the same for all techniques.

The carborundum is always used with running water, so that its particles do not become trapped in the surface of the enamel. Before refiring, the pieces should be rinsed and brushed thoroughly under running water with a glass brush to remove any residue from the stoning process. The piece is then fired for the last time to reglaze the enamel.

Finishing

The final stage is finishing the metal edges. Typically, the edges are polished either mechanically or by hand. Hand-polishing, by burnishing the metal edges or leather buffing, is preferred. It is a lot more labour-intensive, but the technique allows more control.

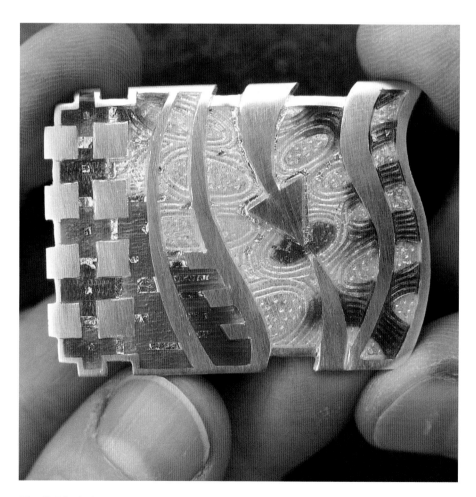

The finished piece

ETCHING

Etching requires the use of acid to remove a layer of metal to form the cells that will hold the enamel. The acid is commonly referred to as a mordant. A resist is applied to protect the areas of metal that do not require etching. There are different kinds of resist. The most familiar is called stop-out varnish. It is a thick, bitumen-like liquid which, when dried off, provides protection from the corrosive action of the acid. Beeswax, sticky-back plastic and graphic resist pens can be used as alternatives, depending on the type of acid used.

A specialist work area is required in order to comply with safety guidelines, as the acids used to etch metal are toxic, very strong and highly corrosive. Acids can be unpredictable and if used carelessly can be extremely dangerous. Further reading on this subject is highly recommended.

The stronger the solution – in other words the greater proportions of pure acid to water – the less controllable the solution is. Strong solutions bite more quickly, but the results may lack refinement. There are different acid solutions that are used to etch silver and copper. The strength of the acid may be varied according to the requirements of the work undertaken. Specialist acid baths can be set up to aid the flow of acid and accelerate processes. Weak acid can take hours or even until the following day to provide the required etch, whereas strong or accelerated solutions may only need 5 to 30 minutes to achieve the desired result.

The common mordants used for each of the metals are described below.

Copper
Ferric nitrate (a solution of one part ferric nitrate to four parts water) or ferric chloride can be used to etch copper. Ferric chloride and ferric nitrate should be dissolved in slightly warm water, following the supplier's instructions, in a well-ventilated space. Ferric chloride can be mixed at different strengths; it is also possible to buy the solution ready-mixed. One part ferric chloride to one part water will allow a quick etch. Weaker solutions can be prepared that will etch much more slowly, allowing more control. This is more suitable for work that has fine detail. Ideally, when etching in ferric chloride or ferric nitrate solution the piece should be suspended upside down as, during the action, the acid biting into the metal creates a residue that should be allowed to fall away from the recesses.

Silver
Nitric acid, or alternatively ferric nitrate, can be used for etching silver. Both are corrosive, but ferric nitrate gives off fewer fumes and is safer to use. Nitric acid is mixed one part nitric acid to three parts water. This is a strong solution. If a

weaker solution is desired the mix should be one part acid to five parts water. Nitric acid is suitable for open areas of an image but will not necessarily give an adequate etch for fine detail, as the action of the acid is fairly strong. It is a very hazardous acid if used incorrectly.

There are a number of health and safety precautions that need to be taken when using acids:

- The acid should be used in a specialist fume cupboard with full ventilation.
- Only ever add acid to water (never vice versa).
- Only mix and store acid in suitable containers (glass or plastic), and label appropriately.
- All safety clothing should be worn: goggles, mask, safety gauntlets, safety apron, solid footwear, etc.
- Baking soda/sodium bicarbonate should be kept to hand to neutralise any potential spillages.
- The acid should be disposed of safely, in accordance with local health authority guidelines.
- Seek immediate medical help in the event of injury or inhalation.

The etching process

The actual etching process is very simple, as described below:

- The metal is thoroughly cleaned and degreased.
- The design is sketched out lightly in pencil.
- The stop-out varnish or resist is then applied and allowed to dry completely. The back and edges of the piece should be thoroughly covered in the stop-out so that the acid only bites the areas that are required.
- Following all safety procedures, the piece is immersed in a shallow dish of acid. The acid should be contained in a suitable container, i.e. plastic or pyrex, and the piece should be handled with plastic

Applying the resist with a paintbrush

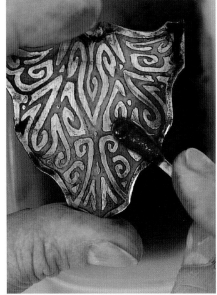

When etching the metal a feather is used to remove bubbles

Removing the stop-out varnish with white spirit

tweezers (not metal). Use only as much acid as you need; some techniques require the piece to be immersed upside down or suspended in vertical tanks. The procedure will vary according to the design requirement.

- The time in acid will likewise vary from a few minutes to half an hour or longer depending on the type and strength of acid coupled with the amount of etch that is needed.
- For *champlevé* enamel an etch depth of 0.2 or 0.3 mm is desirable. The metal used for etched *champlevé* should therefore be of a thicker diameter – around 1.2 to 1.5 mm is the most suitable.
- During the immersion in acid, the piece will require soft brushing with a feather to minimise the formation of bubbles created by the action of the acid, thus ensuring an even bite into the metal.
- Check the depth of etch at intervals – every few minutes if the acid is strong, every 5, 10 or 20 minutes if it is weak. If the cut is not sufficient, return the piece to the acid until the surface is removed to the depth you require.
- On final removal from the acid the piece should be thoroughly washed in water straightaway.
- Ammonia, in a well-ventilated area, can be used to clean and neutralise any residue from the mordant; brushing with sodium bicarbonate will also neutralise any remnant of acid on the metal surface.

- Stop-out varnish can then be removed with white spirit or Polyclens®.
- Once the resist is removed the piece is ready for enamel preparation and/or further treatments.

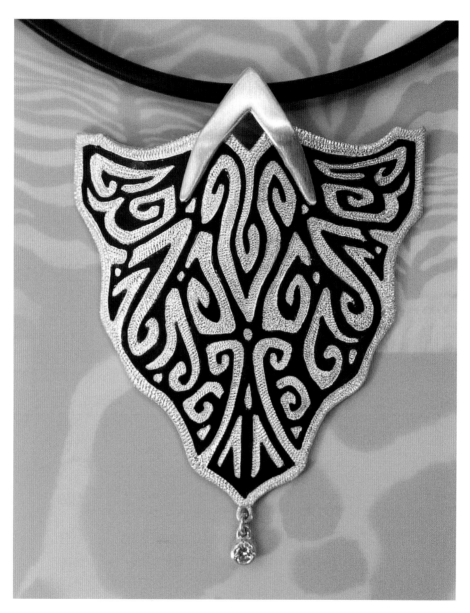

The final enamelled piece fitted to component parts to make a necklace

PHOTO-ETCHING

Photo-etching is a useful method for the production of larger batches of work. The results are very accurate, and it offers a pleasing method for producing multiple images.

The work has to be considered economically as well as in terms of design. The minimum size for commissioning the process is A3. There are charges for production and artwork as well as the cost of a sheet of silver of this size. The basic process requires the image to be produced as a high-quality black and white image. Additional colours for instructional use are red and blue to mark settings for depth or additional requirements. The image is supplied to the photo-etch firm at twice the actual size required. It is best to seek advice from the firm undertaking the etching as to their preferred method. The companies that offer photo-etching are very helpful and will provide a full list of requirements and give advice on the processes involved.

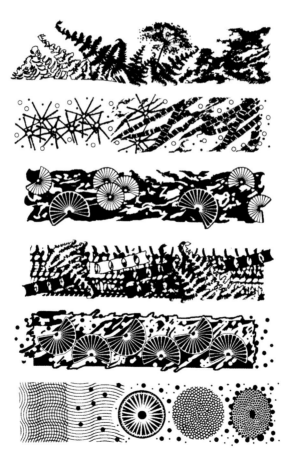

Detail of the black and white artwork. Developed and created in Adobe PhotoShop. Ruth Ball

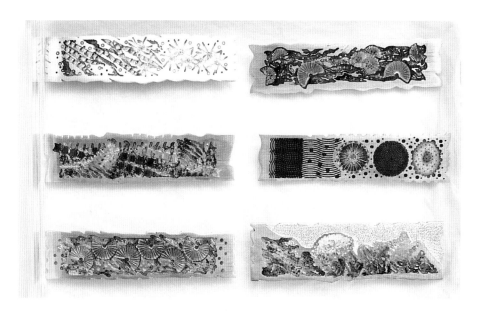

A series of brooches based on water forms by Ruth Ball. Enamel on photo-etched silver. 2.5 × 7 cm (1 × 3 in.). Photo: Ruth Ball.

Blue etching-resist film

This film provides a low-cost method of etching images. It works best when used with high-contrast black and white images that are photocopied. The process also works with laser printers. The film offers an economical option for producing small batches of work in preference to the expense of a larger run of commissioned photo-etched pieces.

Blue etching-resist film also provides the possibility of using a more graphic or photographic type of imagery. Key points to remember for your design are that the black lines are the areas that will resist the acid. They become the raised surface. The remaining areas will be etched away for the placement of enamel. An edge should be designed so that the image can be anchored adequately when attached to the metal, and cut out efficiently once etched. A slow etch is recommended as the film itself is prone to break up in strong solutions. The other major consideration is to remember that images will be reversed, so it is best to check elements that will be affected, i.e. text.

The film comes with full instructions for use and is a reasonably simple method to execute. Basically, the film is fed through the photocopier/laser printer, transferring the image to the film. Once printed, the film is then attached to the metal via the heat from a household iron. The piece is then put through the etching process. After etching, the film can be removed with acetone or Polyclens®, leaving the desired image ready for enamelling.

CHAMPLEVÉ SHOWCASE

The following examples of *champlevé* techniques reflect a strong design element and a graphic approach to imagery.

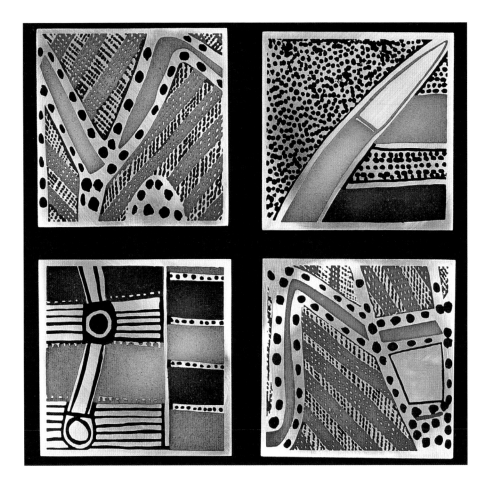

Chameleon Collectable Series, *four brooches by Gudde Jane Skyrme. Silver and enamel. Each brooch 4.5 x 4.5 cm (1¾ x 1¾ in.) square. Photo: Peter White, FXP Photography*

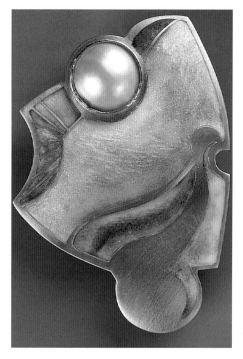

Above: Geometric cufflinks *by Penny Davis, 2003. Enamel on photo-etched silver. 2 × 2 cm (³⁄4 × ³⁄4 in.) diameter. Photo: Penny Davis*

Left: Brooch *by Sarah Letts, 2002. Hand-engraved enamel on silver 18-carat gold and pearl. 4 × 3 cm (1¹⁄4 × 1 in.). Photo: Andra Nelki*

Circles and Squares. *Earrings and necklace set by Jane Moore, 2004. Enamel, photo-etched silver. Largest piece: 5 cm (2 in.) diameter. Photo: David Harban*

Bird brooch *by Jane Short, 2003. Hand-engraved* champlevé/basse taille, *enamel over silver. 7 × 3.5 cm (2¾ × 1¼ in.). Photo: Robert Sanderson*

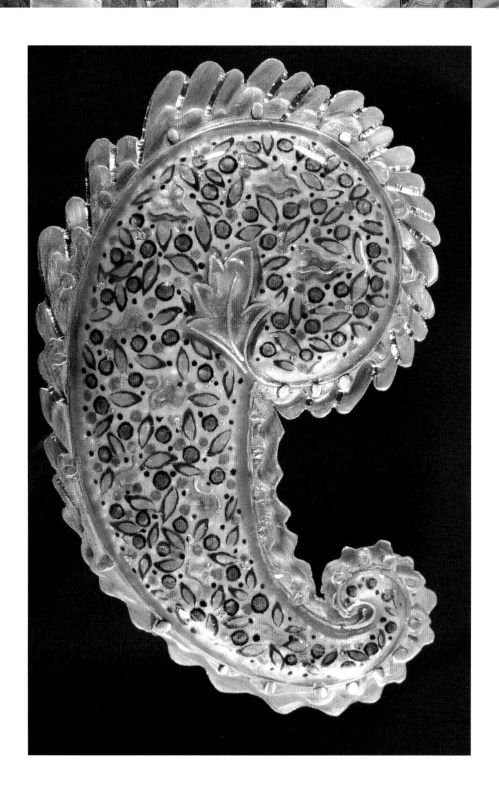

CHAPTER SIX

PAINTED ENAMEL

The painted-enamel method is often referred to as the Limoges technique. Painted enamels consist largely of finely ground metal-oxide pigments. The pigments are painted and fired, typically onto an opaque, white ground coat of enamel, although ground coats other than white may be used. Flux, for example, makes a good base for a variety of applications; it allows for added underplay of texture to be used within the design. Opalescent colours, too, though difficult to control, provide an interesting background. In the *grisaille* painted-enamel technique, very dark grounds (often black or blue) are used as a base for monochrome works.

PAINTED ENAMEL STAGES

Mixing the colours

Although painting enamel is already very fine, after the addition of painting medium, it is reground with a glass muller to a smooth paste. This is done to make sure the paint is of an even consistency and to ensure that it is well mixed. The consistency of the paint is important to the quality and application of the painting.

In the range of paints illustrated on the next page, some of the colours are also mixed and ground with a painted enamel flux. Generally, most enamel painting colours are intermixable, but reds and oranges can be difficult to fire as they will burn out if overfired. The colour is further thinned with the medium when painting, and can be cleaned away with Polyclens®/white spirit.

Paisley brooch by Ruth Ball. Painted enamel on silver.
Photo: Ruth Ball

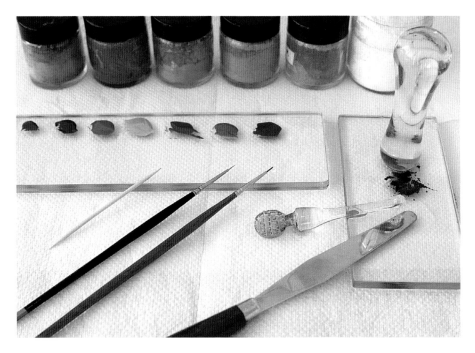

Painted enamel colours mixed using a glass muller

Preparation

For the piece shown in the sample images, the metal was cut to shape, engraved, cleaned and then enamelled with a clear flux. The surface of the metal was lightly engraved with a flinked pattern to give an added texture to the metal. The engraved surface reflects through the painting, adding to the overall design and quality of the work.

Two coats of flux were fired to create a base coat which was lightly stoned. The stoned surface was refired to give an even layer on which to paint. The piece is constructed from silver of 1.5 mm thickness, so no counter-enamel was needed. The fittings were soldered to the reverse of the piece.

Painting the design

Initially, the image for the painting is outlined in a key colour with a fine brush; very fine sable brushes are preferred. The outline is fired into the base coat and acts as a guide for the rest of the work. A painting could, of course, be commenced in a variety of ways; an outline is not completely necessary, but it is used here to demonstrate the idea of building up a design.

The first layer of the painting

Adding more tonal detail to the painting

Firing painted enamel

Painted colours will quickly burn out if overfired, going dull or burning out completely. Initial firing is done cautiously as the layers are fired and built up. Each layer is fired separately, to create a variety of painted effects as needed.

Before firing each layer of painted enamel, the medium, contained and mixed within the paint, must be completely dried. The piece is held just in front of the kiln opening to allow the medium to dry. It is important to give the piece a slow introduction to the full heat of the kiln. Only then, once the vapour from the oil is fully evaporated, should it be fired. On firing, the paint will fuse with the base layer. A piece can be fired many times in order to develop the depth of effects required.

Building up tone

Consecutive layers of enamel are applied and fired, in order to build up tonality in the painting. The outline becomes less obvious and becomes part of the overall effect. Generally, the method used here is to work from light to dark and apply the paint in washes of colour akin to watercolour painting. The pigment should be applied thinly, in fine washes of colour, the brushwork being fairly controlled. Enamel paint will not fire correctly if built up too thickly.

Adding foil and wires

Added decoration, such as foil and extra-fine wires, can be included in the image. Foils and/or fine wires should be added before the flux is applied. Foil and wire are placed with a small amount of gum to hold them in place. The gum is dried off and both the wire and foil are fired together. The fine wire and foil bond with the painted enamel layers.

In the example, tiny gold foil and small snippets of *cloisonné* wire add to the illustrated effect to emphasise and highlight areas, combining to form a painterly finish within the piece.

Adding foils and wires with a paintbrush

Applying finishing flux

Once the fired image is satisfactory, the whole surface of the painting is covered with clear flux and then fired again to give a protective layer and a finished glaze.

Applying clear flux

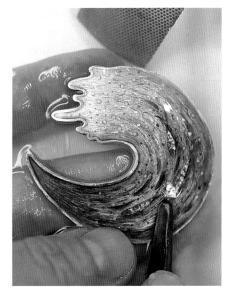

Stoning back

The flux must be ground very finely and washed thoroughly. Any problems at this stage, and hours of painting can be ruined in one firing. The flux must be applied in a very thin coat, thin enough to see the painting through. It is a demanding process and requires particular care and attention to detail.

The image is generally covered with two coats of flux, which are then stoned lightly to give an even finish to the top coat. The piece is then rinsed with a glass brush, as for all methods, to remove any stoning residue, and the piece is refired for the last time.

The flux fuses with the painted enamel colour. It serves not only to give a protective layer, but will also soften and tone down the colours. To counteract this effect, paintings are often executed with more contrast than needed so that on fluxing the colours blend. However, if you get the whole thing wrong the flux can either 'lift' the image or give a milky appearance, and hours of work can be ruined. It is a technique that requires some practice.

The finished piece

THE GRISAILLE METHOD

Grisaille translates as 'greyness' and is a method of painting that employs pure tonality. A dark base coat is covered with consecutive layers of finely ground white enamel to create detailed imaging. Traditionally, black is used as a base for the background, but the effect will work over any dark colour that is of a hard fusibility and will not burn out with repeated firing.

Using extremely finely ground, wet-laid, white opaque enamel can create the tonal effect. Alternatively, white painted enamel pigment with an oil binder (medium) can be used. Finely ground opalescent whites will also give pleasing results. Another technique similar to this is called *'camaieu'*. Instead of a dark base coat, the white overlays are painted over a transparent-coloured base, adding to the range of surface possibilities.

Developing the imagery is basically the same for *grisaille* as if you were using white chalk on black paper. The effects of this technique are striking. It has the potential to be used for a wide range of graphic imagery.

It is important to prepare a good base coat. Before commencing the painting, you should prepare the base coat so that it is of a smooth, even surface and depth. Use hard-fusing enamel, as the piece will be fired several times and will need to carry the white pigment without it affecting the imagery. The image should be built up in layers, and if using painted enamel you will need a coat of clear flux to give it a protective coating and final finish.

An example using the *grisaille* method

A steel, tag-shaped former was press-formed into a sheet of fine silver. The shape was cut out from the sheet and the edges were filed. The recesses pressed into the metal were suitable for enamelling without any further work being needed (i.e. no engraving or etching was required). The resulting tag shape was cleaned, degreased and counter-enamelled.

The front of the tag was covered with two coats of hard black enamel, which was stoned to gain an even surface, washed under running water with a glass brush to remove any residue, and refired to attain a smooth

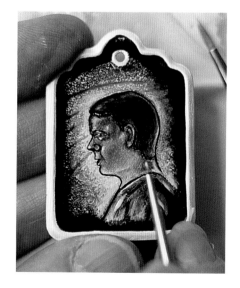

Building up the painting over the black opaque enamel

The final piece

surface. White enamel-painting pigment was painted thinly to sketch out the image and fired.

Consecutive layers of white were applied tonally, and fired between each application to develop the image. When the painting was completed, two layers of finely ground flux were fired over the entire painted surface, which was then stoned back, washed under running water with a glass brush, and refired to provide a final gloss finish to the enamel.

PAINTED ENAMEL SHOWCASE

Painted enamel is traditionally used for very representational work. Highly skilled enamellers create works of exquisite detail. The scope for exploration in this technique is vast, as many types of painted methods can be employed.

Watch case *by Keith Seldon. Painted enamel over 18-carat gold, pearls. Approx. 5.7 cm (2¼ in.) diameter.*

Enamel portrait of Professor David Wray *by Gillie Hoyte Byrom. Enamel on 18-carat gold. 5 × 6.5 cm (2 × 2½ in.). Photo: Alan Cooper Labs*

Homage to the Gecko *necklace by Joan MacKarell, 2003. Painted enamel on silver, agate beads. Painted sections 3.5 × 1.5 cm (1¼ × ¾ in.). Photo: James Austen*

Plique à jour Dragonfly Brooch *by Hali Baykov, 2004. Silver, enamel and precious stones. Approx. 6.5 cm (wingspan) × 7 × 2 cm (3 × 2½ × ¾ in.). Photo: Ruth Ball*

CHAPTER SEVEN

PLIQUE À JOUR

Plique à jour is frequently alluded to as the stained-glass window effect. There are three methods of creating the cell structure for *plique à jour*:

- Piercing a design from sheet metal.
- Soldering wires together to make a framework.
- Fusing wires onto a copper form, which is covered with a flux base, then removing the metal backing via acid etching.

The pierced method is the most straightforward to use. The other two techniques are interesting and ultimately achievable but are much more difficult to master. Using the acid-etch method requires not only a lot of patience but a specialist work area for using acid. The soldered method is an acquired skill and to begin with can be problematic.

Plique à jour requires a lot of initial planning. It is essential, whichever method is employed, to consider the construction of the piece fully before starting the enamel sections. In the design of earrings, a simple hole for the hanging of wire or fittings is sufficient; however, in more complicated sections the screw fitting of sectional parts is desirable.

Sections for Dragonfly Brooch *by Hali Baykov, 2004. Photo: Ruth Ball*

Pale, transparent enamel colours are very suited to *plique à jour*. The lighter the colour, the greater the effect of transparency achieved. Colours should be washed scrupulously, as the clarity of colour is most important. Enamel for *plique à jour* should be ground coarsely (60 mesh or 80 mesh), the grains being like fine sugar or sand in appearance.

THE PIERCED METHOD

As a general guide the main points to consider for the pierced method are as follows:

- Designs for *plique à jour* work best when the apertures for enamel are of equal sizes and are equally spaced. The size of cells should be well structured and the apertures kept small. An even tension is required throughout the piece.
- The shapes of the cells are best kept rounded and free-flowing. Avoid designs with sharp edges, as there will be a greater likelihood of the enamel cracking under surface tension.
- The metal thickness used should be no less than 1.0 mm and no more than 1.5 mm. 1.2 mm is about right.
- Piercing the side wall at an angle will help the enamel fill the pierced structure. The cells will carry the enamel better. Cutting at a slight angle, back-cut with a fine saw blade, cutting the cell wider at the front than the back.
- Use a fine saw blade to cut the cells, in order that the cells can be left unfiled after cutting. A roughened edge will give better adhesion to the enamel.

Firing flat sections of *plique à jour*

For firing flat pieces of *plique à jour*, a sheet of mica is normally used as a support backing in the first and subsequent firings. Mica can be used repeatedly, although after many firings it will break down and flake. It does not adhere fully to the enamel, but residual deposits can still stick to the enamel. Any fired-in sections of mica should be stoned off before the final firing.

It is best to slightly underfire the first coat. The enamel will not fully fill the cells on the first application, and holes and gaps will appear as the enamel peels away. Continue to add subsequent layers of enamel until the cells are filled. Clean any bare metal parts between firing if needed.

Once the cells are full they will require stoning level. This should be done with the greatest of care. The piece should be very well supported, and the minimum of pressure applied in the stoning process. It is also advisable to prepare the finish to the metal edges before the final firing. Hand-finishing to the highest point possible should be done with care, but do not use any polishing compounds on the stoned enamel surface, as the residues from the compounds will remain in the enamel, causing surface imperfections.

Plan the final firing so that the piece can be suspended in some way. Once both sides of the piece have been stoned level the piece should not touch the mica again. The piece should be given a short, high firing just to gloss the enamel surface. Any cracks that have appeared through the stoning process should fire out, leaving a beautiful transparent surface.

An example using the pierced method

The earrings pictured below were cut from a sheet of silver 1.2 mm thick and the cells were marked out in pencil. Holes were drilled at intervals for piercing out with a fine saw blade. A hole that doubled as a fitting point was also designed into the piece to allow for the support of the work on its final firing.

Marking out the cells for the enamel

Piercing the shapes with a fine-bladed jeweller's saw

Filling the cells with well-washed enamels

A sheet of mica supports the enamel when firing

Once fully cut, the silver was degreased and cleaned in pickle. The enamel was ground to about 80 mesh and washed very thoroughly with distilled water. The first coat was underfired and the cells filled very well, but another two layers of enamel were applied.

The piece was then carefully stoned back and the metal edges were given an emery finish. Before being refired, the piece was washed completely with a glass brush under running water to remove any residue from stoning. The piece was given a short, high firing suspended from a wired mesh to give a gloss finish. Finally, the fittings were applied, and no further finishing was required.

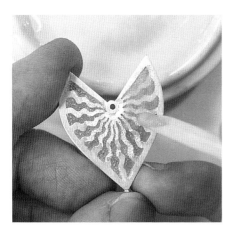

Second coating of enamel to fill up the space in the cells

The piece is suspended on wire mesh in the final firing

THE ACID-ETCH METHOD

More suited to the formation of three-dimensional forms, the acid-etch method is an exacting technique. It is commonly used in the creation of bowls and ornamental goblets. The final effect produced by this method is very beautiful. It is, however, the most fragile of all the techniques and is not often used as a format for jewellery. In simple terms the wires are built up in the manner of *cloisonné* over a metal form covered with clear enamel flux. A copper form is the most commonly used base, as it is the cheapest and easiest to shape. Once the effect is completed the copper backing is etched away, revealing the wires suspended in the surface of the transparent enamel.

In the acid-etch method the key points of the process are given below:

- The copper base shape should be constructed from thin sheet, as it will erode more easily in the acid-etch process. Copper shim is ideal.
- It is important that the copper base metal is scrupulously cleaned and well prepared, as any imperfections will affect the colours.
- An even and solid enamel layer of flux should be fired over the copper, as a foundation layer for the wires. Two to three layers of flux, fired over the copper form, should be applied. If necessary the flux should be stoned and refired to an even surface before the wires are assembled and fired.
- The wires should be rectangular in section, as there needs to be a depth of enamel for the work to attain solidity.

- The wires, as with the pierced method, should be even in structure. The size of cell formed should remain small. Large gaps in the design will create weak spots and increase the potential for the form to crack.
- Once the wires have been fired to the base of flux, the same enamelling procedure is followed as in the *cloisonné* method.
- Transparent enamels should be coarse and very well washed for maximum clarity.
- The piece should be fully stoned and finished from the front face before the removal of the copper base.
- In order to etch away the copper base, a thorough coating of resist/stop-out varnish should be applied to the whole of the front section. Care must be taken that the acid does not lift this protective surface when etching.
- The method of etching will depend on the thickness of your metal, the shape of your object and the strength of acid. Etching should be done with care; a slow etch is preferred.
- Once the copper backing has been removed, the piece should be handled as little as possible, as it will be very fragile.
- Consider carefully how the piece is to be inserted into fittings and finished.
- Rounded shapes are the best forms to use. Sharp or angular designs are not suitable.

As with any technique that requires the involvement of acid, specialist workshop conditions and complete attention to health and safety are paramount. Remember to follow all health and safety procedures when using acid.

THE SOLDERED METHOD

An alternative method involves the soldering of *cloisonné* wire to form a design. It is a highly skilled technique, practised internationally by only a few enamellers.

The solder used should be eutectic solder, or of enamelling quality. Once the form has been soldered, careful attention has to be given to cleaning the piece. Any fire stain present in it must be removed. Solder joints must be very tidy, as excess solder will interact with the enamel, adversely affecting the colour. Enamel is applied using the same technique as is used for the pierced method, with special care taken in the final stages of stoning and firing.

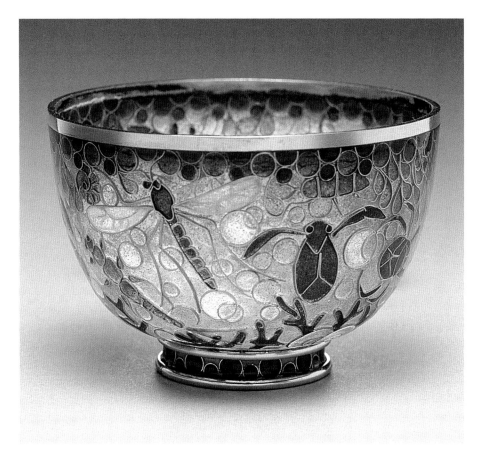

PLIQUE À JOUR SHOWCASE

The elusive transparency of enamel is delicately captured by *plique à jour*. When you have a basic understanding of the process, it is all the more awe-inspiring viewing the virtuosity of the work created by other enamellers.

Pond Life. Plique à jour *bowl by Alexandra Raphael. Enamel and fine gold wires, 18-carat gold rim. 7cm (2¾ in.) high × 10 cm (4 in.) diameter. 'Commended', Goldsmiths Craft Council, 2002. Photo: John Knill*

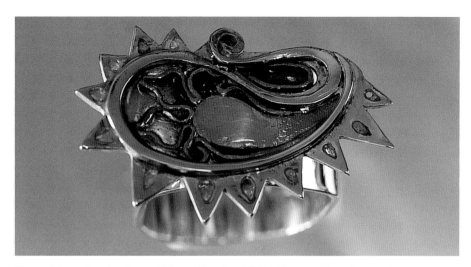

Plique à jour *ring by Jeanne Werge Hartley, 2004. Silver, gold and enamel. 3 × 2 × 2 cm (1¼ × 1 × 1 in.). Photo: Jeanne Werge Hartley*

Work in progress – Face. *Section for* plique à jour *pendant by Sara Bennett, 2005. Enamel on silver-mesh framework. 5 × 7 cm (2 × 2¾ in.). Photo: Sara Bennett*

Plique à jour Butterfly Brooch *by Hali Baykov, 2005. Enamel, silver and precious stones. 5.5 × 6 cm (2 × 2¹/₄ in.). Photo: Ruth Ball*

Multiple test pieces *by Ruth Ball. Enamel on copper and silver.*
Overall size: 42 x 60 cm (16½ x 23½ in.). Photo: Ruth Ball

CHAPTER EIGHT

ADDITIONAL TECHNIQUES

In Chapter 2, sifting is described as a method for grading enamel. In this chapter sifting is the predominant method of applying enamel to metal. Applying the enamel dry though sieves opens up many versatile approaches. Sifting is a simple process. Enamel is placed into the grade of sieve required, and is dusted evenly, through the mesh, onto the metal surface. This chapter also includes liquid enamel, printing methods and the application of foils and leaf. Many of these techniques are considered new and experimental, but, in fact, enamellers have used them for many years.

SGRAFFITO

Sgraffito is a basic method whereby the design is created by scratching through a dry layer of enamel. The groove that is created is fired. The channelled lines that are formed are then filled with a contrasting colour. When stoned back, the marks made reveal the design. The tools used for this method do not have to be specialist pieces of equipment. The best things to use are often household objects such as skewers, knitting needles, combs, old pens, palette knives, cut-up pieces of card, etc. All provide great mark-making opportunities.

Top: Sifting
Bottom: Stages of sgraffito

STENCILLING

Stencilling can be used to provide strong graphic accents. The advantage of stencilling is that designs can be used again. The basic technique involves using an overlay image, through which enamel is sifted, allowing sections of enamel to be dusted onto the surface of the piece.

Stencils can be made in many ways. The easiest is to use found objects that have interesting patterns or open shapes that the enamel will pass through. Alternatively, you can make your own stencils by cutting the shapes from thin paper, card or transparent sticky-back plastic.

Found shapes make useful stencils

USING PENCILS AND PENS

These techniques are very immediate and deserve more exploration. For both techniques a base coat must be fired. It is advisable to fire two coats of base colour then stone back, refiring if necessary to obtain a good surface. The methods work better if the finish is even. For both methods the enamel surface should be dry and grease-free. Opaque enamels work best.

Graphite pencil

Any ordinary pencil will work, and ceramic pencil media will also fire onto a matted enamel surface. Consider the type of mark-making you want to achieve and experiment with the effects that you need.

Before firing, any alterations to your image can be rubbed out with an eraser in the normal fashion. If the marks are very heavy they can be lightly stoned off with carborundum/diagrit.

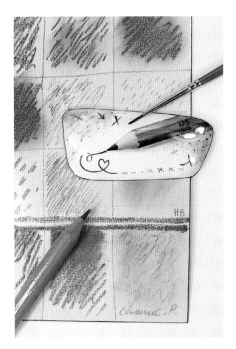

Painted sample and mark-making with pencil

A test piece showing mark-making effects with a fine fibre-tipped pen

The important initial step is in the preparation of the enamel base coat. The surface should be smooth, matted and even. The easiest way of achieving this is to stone the enamel back with a carborundum stone. Applying pencil only works on a matted surface.

Draw directly onto the matted surface and then fire the piece. The image should be drawn more overtoned than needed as some of the strength of line and shading can be lost in firing. Once the piece has been fired it will have a shiny surface. The image can be left at this stage, and will be permanently fired into the enamel surface. The image can also be worked on further if required; however, more firing will cause it to fade. It is possible to add flux to protect the pencil layer, or, alternatively, enamel paint or layers of thin transparent colour can be added for further effect.

Fibre-tipped pens

Drawing over a base coat with fibre-tipped pens is a simple process. The ink in the pen stays wet just long enough to enable the enamel to be sifted over the image marked out. The ink is fired out leaving the particles of enamel on the image.

With this method, the piece needs a smooth base coat of enamel fired to a glossy surface. Once the enamel has cooled, the image is drawn directly onto it. Fine enamel is sifted over the piece immediately, before the ink has time to dry out. A mesh size of 200 or finer works well. Lightly tap the excess enamel off the piece. The enamel should stick to the wet marks made by the pen. You can brush off any remaining enamel in unwanted areas with a fine paintbrush.

Choose pens that will not dry immediately on contact with the enamel. Stay-wet pens or non-permanent wipe-board markers work well. The ink colour in the pen will fire away, so the colour of the pen itself is not important; simply choose a colour that will show up well for you when you are drawing. The enamel colour that is sifted over the marks you make is the colour that will fire. The base enamel should ideally be a medium- or high-firing colour.

Fire the piece gently. With the enamel being fine, the layer will not take long to fire into the base enamel. Be careful not to overfire as the drawing may burn out, or may soften too much into the enamel base coat. The image can be left as it is or a flux layer can be applied if needed; alternatively, the process can be repeated, building up a variety of effects within the image. Repeated firing may alter initial coats, but with careful control a certain depth of imagery can be achieved.

PAINTING WITH GUM SOLUTIONS

A simple method of painting an image is to brush thin applications of a gum solution directly onto a base layer of enamel. There are several products that can be used. Klyre fire, gum tragacanth or enamel-paint medium all work well. Klyre fire is thinner in consistency than enamel-paint medium and will take less enamel on sifting.

Other solutions can be used. Some experimentation can be achieved with art products not normally associated with enamel, e.g. food colouring, embossing fluid, System 3 acrylic medium, glycerol and diluted wallpaper paste. The most important factor is that the solution used should be organic and non-toxic. It should burn away in the kiln and not affect the quality of the enamel.

- Using your preferred solution paint your marks over the enamel surface using a brush.
- Sift dry enamel over the image you have created. Use 100 mesh or finer (the finer meshes work better with this method). Tip off any excess enamel and tidy the image with a dry paintbrush if needed.
- Dry off any moisture and then fire the piece. The image can be left as it is or the process can be repeated as necessary, building up layers of marks, patterns or images.

The effects can require some control and manipulation of technique, as fine layers of enamel can burn out with repeated firing. The colours used will determine the outcome. For example, if you want to fire a red, leave it until the last firing, as reds have a tendency to burn out.

PRINTING WITH RUBBER STAMPS

You can make you own rubber stamps easily, by drawing and cutting an image into a rubber eraser. The printing method is simple and straightforward, allowing the possibility of creating repeat images. There are two ways of applying the enamel:

- You can stamp using enamel paints. Spread enamel paint onto a tile and smooth it out with a roller. Ink up the rubber stamp and stamp directly onto the surface of smooth enamel.
- You can stamp using a clear embossing pad (which may be purchased from craft stores), and then sift the dry enamel over the dampened printed surface.

The image can be printed and fired just once, or layers of stamped images can be fired to build up interesting aspects to the design. Each method of stamping will give a slightly different effect; much will depend on the style, the colour range you require and what you have available.

Printing with painted enamel using a rubber eraser

SCREENPRINTING

Images can be applied to enamel via traditional silk-screenprinting methods. Riso screens, produced using a thermal imager machine, create an adequate screen that can be used with great ease. This method is more often used to create panel work, but it also offers great opportunities for jewellery designs.

Riso screen is a light-sensitive material that reacts with photocopy toner when fed through a special heated light source. Black and white photocopies of your image should be of a high contrast. The thermal imager is similar in size to a domestic computer printer. The material placed into the carrier is fed through the machine, which burns the image onto the Riso material. It is an extremely quick process, similar in timescale to the photocopying of your original image.

For the Riso-screen method, the enamel is always applied in dry powder form. The Riso-screen material is not compatible with oil-based media, or the cleaning products used with oils. White spirit and the like will lift the screen emulsion and ruin the image. Riso screens should only be cleaned with water, or simply dusted with a clean paintbrush to remove excess powder.

Pushing fine enamel through a Riso screen with a sponge

To apply the enamel through the screen, the enamel is sifted through or pulled through the screen with a piece of card or soft sponge. The application of enamel is aided by painting the surface of the enamel with a thin and evenly applied coating of Klyre fire before printing, to give a tacky surface for the enamel to fall onto.

Once applied the enamel is fired in the normal way; different layers of printing can be applied and fired in order to build up an image. Finely ground enamel works best, although there are variations in the grain size that can be used.

USING LIQUID ENAMEL

More commonly, liquid enamel is associated with industrial enamel applications. Available in a range of colours, it has become an interesting material with which to extend the methods available in enamel.

Liquid enamel is used with copper or steel. It can be applied to the metal in a range of methods including dipping, spraying or pouring, or it can be painted onto the metal with brushes. It is useful for sgraffito, slip trailing and a range of more painterly styles. Liquid enamel has a very fine particle size, which enables finely detailed work to be performed, particularly when it is being used with the sgraffito method.

*Coating
copper
shapes with
liquid enamel*

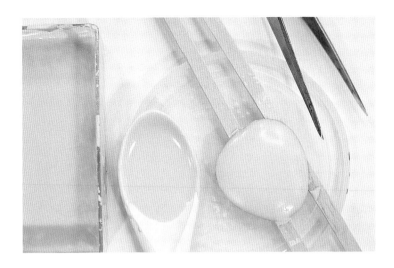

Liquid enamel, like all other enamels, should be applied in even coats. The consistency of the liquid is similar to thin single cream. If the mixture is too thick water can be added to thin the solution. If it has become hard or has dried out completely it can be covered with a layer of hot water, which will be reabsorbed by the powder. It can then be mixed with more water as necessary until the correct consistency is acquired.

To cover a piece entirely with liquid enamel the article is simply dipped into the solution. The piece is removed using tweezers, allowing the coating to drip off evenly. The piece can be rotated if needed to obtain a consistent layer. The piece is then left to dry, supported over a lid or similar to catch any dripping enamel. Alternatively, liquid enamel can be brushed on, either initially or at later stages in the development of the piece.

It should be noted that liquid enamel should be fully dry before it is fired. Firing is the same for all the other techniques. Three-dimensional objects that are coated both sides should be fired on a trivet rather than directly over the mesh.

Painting with liquid enamel

USING FOILS AND LEAF

The application of fine-carat gold or silver foil can give added dimension to the enamel surface. Gold and silver foils and leaf can be applied over any base coats, transparent or opaque. Any protective layers of enamel over foil must be a transparent colour or a flux.

Foil and leaf are different to each other in thickness, and thus are applied and fired differently. Foil is applied to a base coat and needs a subsequent layer of enamel to provide protection and finish. Leaf can be fired onto a final coat of enamel and will fuse into the enamel as a finished effect.

Foil

Foil can be bought in different thicknesses. It is thicker than leaf and can be picked up with tweezers. It is applied with a fine brush. It can be cut with a scalpel blade or scissors, or alternatively, craft punches can be used to create uniform geometric shapes. The best method for doing any of the cutting operations is to keep the foil sandwiched between two layers of tracing paper.

Before cutting the required shapes it is also advisable to pierce tiny holes into the foil to perforate the surface. If air becomes trapped under the foil when it is fired, holes will appear and the enamel may chip, firing unsatisfactorily. The foil can be pierced with a fine sewing needle, but the most effective method of piercing a foil sheet is to perforate using a fine emery sheet. To do this, place the emery sheet gently over the foil. Gently rub the back of the emery sheet with

Cutting foils with craft tools

Applying
gold leaf

firm pressure, using your fingers or the palm of your hand. Remove the emery sheet, and, although the perforations will not be visible, the sheet will have become finely pitted.

To apply the foil, position it using a fine paintbrush dipped in water. If you use any type of gum, this can lead to residual problems when the foil is fired. The gum will not evaporate as efficiently as water, and can become trapped under the foil whilst being fired. Once the foil is laid down into position, any moisture is dried off and the piece is then lightly fired in the kiln. The foil will sink very slightly into the enamel layer when fired. Take care not to overfire, as the foil can burn away.

Next, a protective layer of enamel should be applied to bond the foil. Applying more enamel also creates extra interest, either decoratively or as part of the colour range of the design. If you add a coloured transparent over the foil it will reflect the colour through the enamel however, if you require the foil to stay gold (or silver) in colour, use clear flux as the overlay.

Leaf

Leaf is extremely fine. Cutting leaf into shape is very difficult, even between paper sheets. Lifting it by hand is impossible, as it has a tendency to cling to everything, liberally coating everything it touches. Leaf can be fired within layers of enamel, but it burns away much more readily than foil, so is best applied in the final firings of a piece. It does not need a protective coating as it bonds integrally into the enamel. Each firing breaks up the leaf, which can lead to very interesting, if unpredictable, results.

Perforation of leaf is not needed or possible, as it is such a fine layer of metal. Placing the leaf over the work requires a little practice, as at first it will just fall where it wants to! It can be manipulated, though, by scratching through or rubbing off before firing. Once fired into the enamel it can also be stoned back for additional effect, although it will continue to change its appearance on each subsequent firing.

To apply leaf, first brush the area you want to cover with a fine layer of water. Pick up the leaf with a clean, slightly damp paintbrush. Lift the leaf carefully and place it over your enamelled area. Using the paintbrush, position the leaf, carefully patting it down. Scratch through or rub away any areas required to emphasise your design. Dry off any moisture in the door of the kiln and then fire. The leaf fuses with the enamel and will break into the surface of the enamel, creating an antique effect. This effect is best done as a final finish, although it can also be fired and worked on further. However, the effect will alter after every firing as the gold burns out.

WORKING ON COPPER WITH OXIDES UNDER FLUX

The entrapment and control of copper oxide with a clear enamel flux produces interesting effects. The technique can be used for pattern and textural combinations. Alternatively, with learned control, it can be equally useful as a method of acquiring subtle illustrative effects.

The range of colours achievable with flux and copper is determined by the level of oxide present in the copper and the temperatures that the piece is exposed to. By applying oxide barriers such as auflux, borax or scalex to the metal on heating, the surface of the metal and the levels of oxide within it can be controlled. Variations can be achieved by cleaning specific areas and leaving

Clear flux over fold-formed, pressed shapes revealing the oxide colours in the copper

others with the surface blackened through heating. Drawing through an unfired layer of flux, then firing, will produce blackened lines in the enamel surface. A further sifting and firing of flux will colour the lines red, brown or black, depending on the level of firing.

The colours achievable range from golden coppery hues to deep-red and brown patinas. Generally, if the copper is well cleaned and has not been heated, the flux fires a coppery yellow on a high firing. Once the copper has been introduced to heat, and therefore oxide, the colours that flux creates will vary. Initially, you will have to experiment to understand the process and develop a personal style. The art to this technique lies in its simplicity and in the control of temperatures.

SALT-AND-PEPPER EFFECTS

Enamel is conventionally used in solid, flat colours; however, there are two methods of achieving speckled effects in enamel.

- Fire a hard-fusing colour over a contrasting soft-fusing one. The softer colour interfuses with the surface, giving a mottled or speckled effect.
- Use two contrasting colours that have the same fusing rate. Grind or sieve them separately to a coarse grain size, around 60 or 80 mesh. The two enamels can be applied either by sifting or wet-laying methods. The enamel particles will fuse together, but each individual grain will be visible, producing an interesting variation of surface.

Salt-and-pepper effect test piece. Contrasting opaque colours over copper

ADDITIONAL TECHNIQUES SHOWCASE

Experimentation with innovative techniques can produce richly developed and varied work in enamel. The work here is just a small taste of the wealth of creative possibilities.

Brooch *by Ann Little. Enamel, silver, gold, copper, mother-of-pearl and gold leaf. 5 × 5.5 cm (2 × 2¼ in.). Photo: Graham Clark*

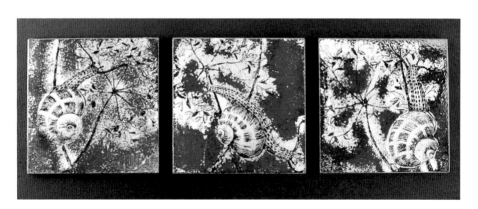

Snail Trio. *Triptych panel by Deirdre McCrory, 2004. Enamel flux over copper. Each panel: 10 × 10 cm (4 × 4 in.). Photo: Deirdre McCrory*

Gold Ceremonial Drinking Bowl *by Marilyn Druin. Enamel, 24-carat gold, fine silver, hand-raised bowl. Photo: Mel Druin*

Sift series. *Three brooches by Jessica Turrell, 2002. Silver, enamel on copper. 4.5 cm (1¾ in.) diameter. Photo: Jessica Turrell*

CHAPTER NINE
TROUBLESHOOTING

The most common enamel complaints involve firing difficulties and initial preparation. Either the enamel or the metal was inadequately cleaned or the piece was overfired. The most common problems are described below.

Acid sensitivity

Some colours are sensitive to pickle, both sulphuric acid and safety pickle. If affected the surface of the enamel gains a milky sheen. If the enamel is very susceptible to this it can even become dull and pitted.

Balled-up patches

When too much enamel is applied the enamel will 'gather up on itself', returning to its glassy, fritlike state. If the enamel is applied unevenly, where the greater amount of enamel is placed more balling up occurs.

Balled-up patches

Bare patches

Damp enamel will evaporate rapidly if it is not dried off properly before being placed into the kiln. As patches of moisture evaporate, the enamel will come off, leaving the metal surface exposed to the heat of the kiln.

Blisters

A blister is a large bubble that will cause the enamel to pop off. The most common cause of blisters is applying too thick a layer of enamel, and not drying it off properly. The inadequate cleaning of the metal, or oxides or impurities in the metal itself, as well as grease, unrinsed acid deposits and overuse of holding agents can also form blisters.

Bubbles

Tiny bubbles in transparent colours tend to appear when the piece is not dried sufficiently before it is fired. In wet-packing techniques, the piece should be lightly tapped before drying off. Similar bubbles, which become clusters of little craters in opaque colours, are also caused by incorrect application of enamel.

This is more common in the wet-laying technique, as if the enamel is not evened out when tapping, the moisture in the enamel is trapped, forming air pockets. Other causes of bubbles include overfiring certain colours, adding too much holding agent or using old enamel that has deteriorated.

Burnt-out patches

Dark or altered colour patches in the enamel are almost always developed when the layer of enamel is applied unevenly and overfired. It may not be possible to salvage the work, as the patch formed will continue to reveal itself in the surface of the enamel. Conversely, some colours can be quite interesting when they are high-fired. You could experiment to control and develop the effects you find inspiring. Note also that if you overfire your piece it may also have an adverse effect on the piece's metal parts. If you overfire significantly, the wires in *cloisonné* will melt.

Cloudy colour

When transparent enamel becomes cloudy or milky on firing, the causes are either that the enamel or the metal was not cleaned properly or that the enamel has deteriorated.

Colour change

Colour changes can be caused by overfiring or by inadequate stoning. Some opaque colours are particularly sensitive to the surface changes that occur on stoning. A subtle colour difference is occasionally noted when a piece has been lightly stoned. If you only stone back the high areas and leave the low areas shiny, when you refire, the matted areas will fire to a slightly different tone of colour. This is because the enamel that is matt through stoning has refired at a different rate to the enamel that had already attained a glossy state.

Cracking

There are several reasons why enamel may crack. It is prudent to remember that enamel is glass. If it is dropped the surface will be exposed to damage. If cooled down too quickly, the rapid thermal change will cause great stress to the enamel and the metal, which will result in the surface cracking into multiple fissures, or even causing the enamel to pop off dramatically from the piece. If the balance between the metal thickness and the counter enamel is not correct for the size and shape of the piece, cracking will occur. Incompatibility between enamels of

Cracking

differing fusing characteristics is another likely cause of cracking. If the piece is too cold when it enters the kiln it is more likely to crack. It is always advisable to warm the piece in the open door of the kiln before firing fully. If you have removed the enamel from the kiln before the colour reglazes you will sometimes see small cracks in the enamel, which, when fired more fully will reglaze into the surface. One other possible reason for cracks could be impurities in the metal.

Dark edges

If the edges of your enamel are darkened or black, this suggests the enamel was overfired. Some colours are more prone to this than others. Reds in particular burn out very quickly. The edge tends to blacken first, as the enamel is thinner at this section.

Discoloured patches

Patches of discolouration are normally the result of grease, either from incorrect cleaning or more typically from the enamel area being touched whilst the enamel itself is being applied. Finger grease deposited into the enamel becomes a contaminant and will appear as a dull or cloudy area. The problem is more apparent in transparent colours. Areas of fire stain in silver will also have an adverse effect on the enamel. If the problem is linked to fire stain, the patches may chip off.

Fire stain

Fire stain is the name given to the oxidised layer produced in standard silver and some gold alloys. Fire stain in the metal should be removed before the piece is enamelled, as it will cause imperfections in the enamel finish.

Shorelines

Water-like marks can become present in the enamel if it has been touched up at some point on subsequent firings. Differences in the firing of the enamels that are used may result in the appearance of fine, dull lines of colour.

Salt and peppering

This is a phenomenon that depends on the interaction of colours on firing. It is not a flaw as such, but should be regarded as a particular characteristic of firing a high-fusing colour over a colour of low fusibility. The result can be quite interesting, although the effects do require some control in order to look refined.

Salt and peppering

Specks/spots/pinholes

Fine specks or larger spots in the enamel can have several causes, such as fire stain, contamination from dust and dirt, deteriorated enamel, or enamels that were not washed properly. They can also be caused by enamel that has transferred from one section to another (this happens on firing if the piece has not been dried off completely).

Warpage

Enamel expands and contracts at a different rate to the metal that it is fusing to. Any imbalance in the tension arising from the bonding that takes place will result in the piece becoming warped. This effect can be minimised by careful planning in the design of your piece. The metal parts should be of the correct thickness to the design requirements and, if needed, counter enamel should be applied.

REMEDY AND REPAIR

To improve a finish that has gone wrong, you will first need to decide on the cause of the defect.

- If the defect is on the top surface of the enamel, you can stone back the enamel and refire.
- Spots, bubbles or blisters should be pricked open with an engraving tool (wear safety goggles/visor). The area should be rinsed with a glass brush under running water to remove any particles, and then refired. More enamel should be applied to regain the enamel surface.
- If the piece is cracked or chipped, counter enamel may be needed to balance the tension in the metal.
- If the flaw is in the metal, or if the surface is badly affected, sometimes the best thing to do is to remove the enamel and start again. The metal or enamels may need to be cleaned more effectively.

The repair of commercial items should only be tackled if you know the exact cause of the problem. It is very difficult to match or replace colours. The enamel normally needs to be removed and reapplied. To remove enamel it needs to be etched away. The chemical used, hydrofluoric acid, is extremely dangerous and highly corrosive – avoid inhalation and contact with skin, bone and fabrics. It should only ever be used in a controlled environment, strictly adhering to Health and Safety guidelines. Further reading on this topic is recommended. Always check the construction of the article. Lead solder should not be used for repairs to metal parts.

CHAPTER TEN

GALLERY

More of enamel's intriguing qualities, embodied in the works of national and international enamellers, are profiled over the next pages. The images selected serve to identify the wide range of ideas and styles that are possible.

JEWELLERY

Earrings *by Ann Little, 2001. Silver, slate, enamel, 18-carat gold. 2/1.5 cm (¾ in.). Photo: Graham Clark*

Opposite: Graffiti Brooch *by Penny Davis, 2003. Silver and enamel. 5.5 x 2.3 cm (2¼ x 1 in.). Photo: Penny Davis*

Connected Wires. Moebius Ribbon Pendant *by Renate Riedel-Anacker. Enamel and silver. 7.5 × 4.4 cm (3 × 1½ in.). Won the Silver Award for Excellence, La Pola, Tokyo, 1998. Photo: Renate Riedel-Anacker*

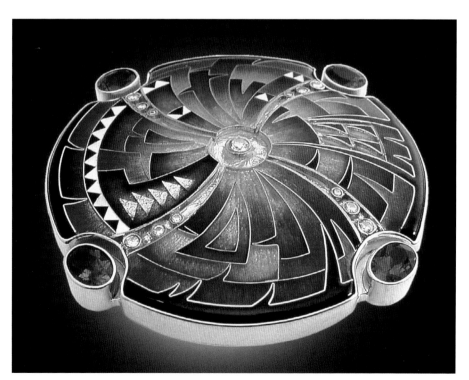

Cloisonné Brooch *by Magic, 2003. 18-carat gold, diamonds, garnets and enamel. 7.5 × 7.5 cm (3 × 3 in.). Photo: Falcher Fusager*

Geometric
Brooches *by*
Jane Short,
2000.
Champlevé
enamel and
silver. Approx.
6 cm (2½ in.).
Photo: Robert
Sanderson

Pendant *by Annie Appleyard, 2003.*
Photo-etched silver, gold foil, cloisonné
wire and enamel. 5 cm (2 in.) diameter.
Photo: Nick Hall

Black and White Sculptural Pendant *by*
Erica Druin, 2004. Collaboration with
Michael Good. Enamel, gold foils and
silver. 4.5 × 4.5 × 4.5 cm (1¾ × 1¾ × 1¾
in.). Photo: Ralph Gabriner

The use of enamel is not solely confined to jewellery. Many types of object have been enamelled, both historically and today. Enamel is used to embellish small domestic items as well as pieces that are of architectural scale.

LARGE PANELS

Facilities for large-scale enamel works are not widely available, as the creation of large panels requires industrial methods of production. In the making of such panels, the enamel is generally applied in liquid form with a spray gun, but can also be sifted onto smaller sections. The panels are made of steel or copper.

Large panel by Pat Johnson. Enamel on steel. Photo: Pat Johnson

When being fired, the pieces are loaded onto a long, rolling, flat-bedded trivet, which enters a large industrial kiln. In this method of firing, several pieces are fired at once; the production of such work is more factory-orientated.

Large industrial kiln. Photo: Pat Johnson

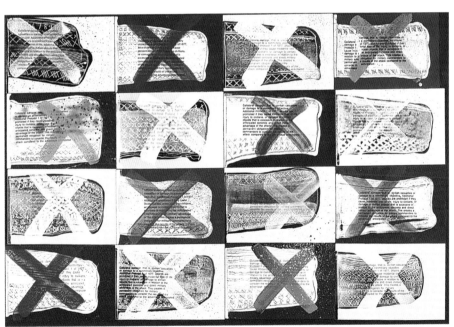

Collateral Damage. *Panel from the 'Universal Declaration of Human Rights' series by Elizabeth Turrell, 2001. Enamel on steel. 60 × 41 cm (24 × 16 in.). Photo: Elizabeth Turrell*

SMALL PANELS

Smaller panels can be produced using more conventional techniques and fired in standard kilns. The size of the piece made will depend on the size of the kiln available. If larger sections are desired, pieces can be designed to fit together in sections, or may be worked on as a series of linking images.

Her Growing Season. *Panel by Morgan Brig, 2004. Enamel, copper and mixed media. Overall size: 58.5 x 35.5 x 7.5 cm (23 x 14 x 3 in.). Photo: Christopher Conrad*

'Sampler' series. *Panel by Hilary Bolton, 2004. Copper and enamel. 18 × 12 cm (7 × 5 in.). Photo: Hilary Bolton*

'Garland' series. *Panel by Ulla Huttunen. Copper, silver foil, enamel and wood. 16 × 16 cm (6½ × 6½ in.). Photo: Ulla Huttunen*

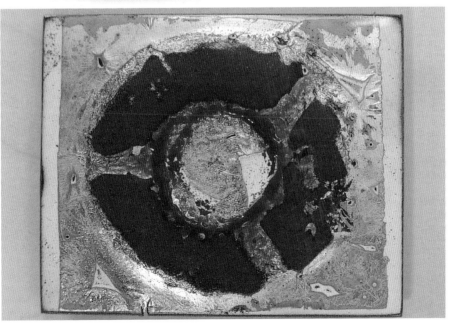

BOWLS AND VESSELS

Enamelled bowls typically utilise shape and form together with colour and surface texture. This combination provides stunning results.

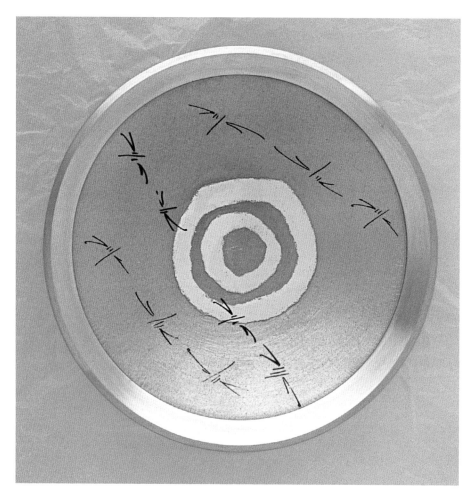

Continuum. *Dish by Sarah Wilson. Enamel and silver. 9.5 cm (4 in.) diameter.*
Photo: Rodney Forte

Jewish
Ceremonial Cup
(Kiddush Cup) *by*
Tamar De Vries
Winter, 2002.
Enamel and silver.
7 cm (3 in.) high
× 6.2 cm (2½ in.)
diameter. Private
collection.
Photograph:
James Austin

Bowls by Vladimir Bohm, 2004. Hand-raised. Enamel and silver.
Largest: 18 × 18 cm (7 × 7 in.). Photo: Andra Nelki

OBJECTS

Objects in enamel are diverse. In the past enamel was used for many different types of item, from religious icons to small boxes and trinket novelties. The role of the enamel can be both decorative and functional.

Chess pieces *by Alan Mudd, 1993. Made from silver which has been enamelled and gold plated. Height: 8 cm (3¼ in.).*
Photo: Gordon Olley, LMPA, Breckland Photographic

Two salts with spoons, *by Ros Conway. Encrusted enamel, fine gold wire and gold leaf on electroformed fine silver. 16 × 8 × 6.5 cm (6½ × 3 × 2½ in.). Collection: Richard Cobbold and Worshipful Company of Goldsmiths. Photo: Ros Conway*

Church Font *by Allan Heywood. Enamel, copper-silver plated and gold wires/foils. 61.5 cm (24 in.) diameter. Commissioned for the Mary Immaculate Mother of God Roman Catholic Church, Bellingen, NSW, Australia. Photo: Allan Heywood*

SCULPTURE

Sculptural forms allow enamel to be utilised in a wider, art-based context. In commissioned works of public art-enamel is dynamic. It has the added benefit of being resilient to the weather. Colour in enamel is permanent and will never fade.

Wall sculpture by Francisco Porras. Copper mounted on stainless-steel sheet and Plexiglas®. Approx. 80 x 80 cm (31½ x 31½ in.). Photo: Francisco Porras

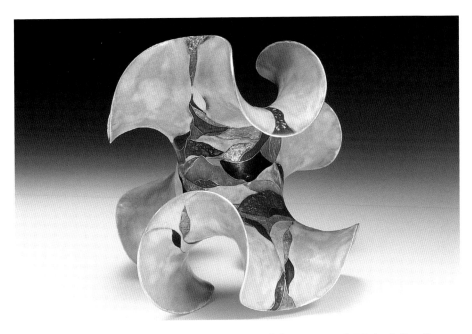

Waving Boundaries. *Sculpture by Erica Druin (collaboration with Michael Good). Enamel, 24-carat gold and fine silver. 11.5 × 11.5 × 9.5 cm (4½ × 4½ × 3¾ in.). Photo: Ralph Gabriner*

Wall Sculpture *by Francisco Porras. Enamelled copper shapes mounted onto steel forms, over an iron frame. Approx. 120 × 80 cm (48 × 32 in.). Photo: Francisco Porras*

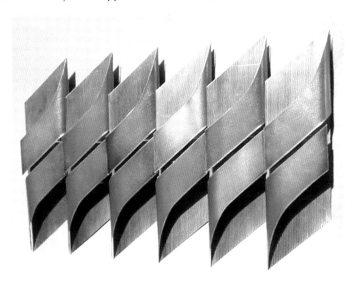

GLOSSARY

Annealing: the process of heating metal to soften its structure, making it more malleable.
Alloy: a mixture of metals.
Auflux: a solution used when soldering or as an oxide inhibitor.
Aqueous: suspended in water.

Basse taille: a transparent enamel technique in which the metal is engraved to show a pattern or image through the surface of the enamel.
Burnisher: a polished metal tool used for brightening metal edges and securing settings.
Ball clay: a slip clay used as on oxide inhibitor (also called scalex) or brushed on kiln supports to prevent enamel sticking when firing in the kiln.

Camaieu: a painting technique in which tonal images are painted over coloured transparent backgrounds.
Counter-enamel: the layer of enamel applied to the back of an article, which prevents warping.
Champlevé: a method whereby enamel is placed into engraved or etched depressions in the surface of the metal.
Cloisonné: a method that uses fine wires to create the areas for enamel.
Chasing: a method of creating shapes in relief using punches.
Carborundum: an abrasive compound used for stoning enamel to a smooth surface.

Decals: images that are made into transfers, which can be applied to the enamel.
Dry applications: a term for sifting, stencilling and scraffito.

Engraving: the process of cutting away the metal surface with specialist tools.
Etching: a method of removing a layer of metal using acid.
Engine turning: a machine method of using lathes to create complex, brightly engraved surface patterns.

Fire stain: an oxidising layer in metal.
Flux: a clear transparent enamel.
Frit: rough chunks of enamel. Also called lump.
Fines: extremely fine grain sizes of enamel.
Flinked: a texture created with a half-round engraving tool.

Wild Necklace, *Annie Appleyard, 2004. Fine silver, 18-carat gold, enamel with jasper, silver and shell beads. 6 x 2 cm (2½ x ¾ in.). Photograph: Nick Hall*

Grinding: the term for crushing and milling down enamel in a pestle and mortar.

Grissaille: a tonal painted enamel technique, normally black and white.

Glass brush: a glass fibre brush used for cleaning metal.

Holding agent: a gum solution used to keep enamel in place before firing.

Klyre fire: an organic solution used as a gum.

Lead-bearing enamel: enamel that contains lead.

Limoges enamel: a reference to painted enamel techniques.

Limoges: a town in France famous for the painted enamel method.

Lump enamel: chunks of enamel. Also called frit.

Lustres: liquid metallic oxides that can be fired into the enamel surface for decorative effect.

Liquid enamel: finely ground enamel that is suspended in an aqueous solution combined with special additives.

Millefiore: small decorative glass elements.

Mica: a flat sheet support used for firing plique a jour enamel.

Mordant: a corrosive solution used for etching acid.

Opaque: solid enamel colour

Opalescent: enamel with a milky or an iridescent characteristic.

Overglaze: painted enamel, which can be fired onto the top, layered surface.

Oxidised layer: a layer of metal alloy that forms a discoloured/darkened surface in the metal when heated or exposed to air over time.

Trilogy, *Erica Druin. Hand-raised beads with 24-carat gold cloisonné and* basse taille *enamel on fine silver with hand-formed 18-carat gold suspension links. Largest component: 7.5 x 2 x 2 cm (2⁷/₈ x ³/₄ x ³/₄ in.). Photograph: Richard Goodbody*

Painted enamel: enamel pigment that is mixed with oils to a paste suitable for painting.

Pickle: an acid based solution used to clean and remove oxide in metals.

Plique à jour: a method of creating transparent enamel that has no backing, the design is viewed from both sides.

Press-form: a technique in which shapes are created by exerting high pressure on a metal through cut out forms.

Pyrometer: a gauge to measure kiln temperature.

Repoussè: a method of shaping metal, using punches over a pitch base.

Assorted found objects, suitable for stencilling

Sifting: the term for applying enamel using sieves.

Stencilling: a method for creating a design by sifting enamel through pre-formed shapes or cut out designs.

Sgraffito: a method of scratching through layer/s of enamel.

Scalex: the product name for ball clay, a slip like substance that is used as an oxide inhibitor.

Stop out: a varnish that is acid resistant.

Stoning: filing with an abrasive material to smooth out the enamel surface.

Thread: very fine enamel rods that have been pulled into thin threads from a molten state.

Trivet: a device for supporting work.

Transparent: coloured enamels that allow light to shine though, revealing the metal surface.

Underglaze: enamel paints that require a clear flux coating.

Underfired: enamel that is not fired to maturity, granular in finish.

Warping: distortion in the metal due to heating and the differing expansion rate of enamel and metal.

Zinc: a white metal alloy.

DIRECTORY

UK SUPPLIERS

Enamel and sundries

Vitrum Signum
Diatherm and Ancillary Equipment
Gresham Works
Mornington Road
North Chingford
London E4 7DR
Tel: 020 8524 9546
www.vitrumsignum.co.uk
All enamels, kilns, wires, foils, leaf, etc.

The Enamel Shop
Trethinnia House
Trethinnia, Altarnun, Launceston
Cornwall PL15 7SY
Tel: 01266 880092
Electric kilns, all supplies.

Milton Bridge
Unit 9 Trent Trading Park
Bottleslow Street
Hanley, Stoke on Trent ST1 3NA
Tel: 01782 274229
www.milton-bridge.co.uk

W.G. Ball Ltd
Anchor Road
Longton
Stoke on Trent ST3 1JW
Tel: 01782 312286
www.wgball.com
Liquid enamels/enamel supplies.

Photo-etching

Chempix (Division of Precision Micro Ltd)
PO Box 162
30 Curzon Street
Birmingham B4 7XD
Tel: 0121 359 5623 or 0121 359 4474
www.chempix.com

Decals

Pamela Moreton Ceramics
22d Holt Road, Cromer
Norfolk NR27 9JW
Tel: 01263 512629
pmc_cromer@lineone.net
www.pmoretonceramics.co.uk
Ceramic transfers etc.

Kilns

Northern Kilns
Pilling Pottery
School Lane
Nr Garstang
Lancashire PR3 6HB
Tel: 01253 790307
www.northernkilns.co.uk

Kilns and Furnaces Ltd
Cinderhill Trading Estate
Weston Coyney Road
Longton
Stoke on Trent
Staffordshire S3 5JU
www.kilns.co.uk

Precious metals

Cookson Precious Metals
49 Hatton Garden
London EC1N 8YS
Tel: 020 7400 6500
www.cooksongold.com
Bullion, gold, silver, platinum, chain,
findings, sundries, tools

J Blundell & Sons Ltd
31-35 Leather Lane
London EC1 7TE
Tel: 020 7404 0744
www.jblundell.co.uk
Bullion, gold, silver, platinum, chain,
findings, sundries, tools

Tools

H.S. Walsh
Head Office - 243 Beckenham Rd
Kent BR3 4TS
Tel: 020 8778 7061
www.hswalsh.com
Tools, equipment, sundries, findings.

Precious stones

Marcia Lanyon Ltd
PO Box 370
London W6 7NJ
Tel: 020 7602 2446
www.marcialanyon.co.uk

R. Holt & Co. Ltd
98 Hatton Garden
London EC1N 8NX
Tel: 020 7405 5286
www.holtsgems.co.uk
www.rholt.co.uk

US SUPPLIERS

Thompson Enamel, Inc.
PO Box 310
Newport
KY 41072
Tel: (859) 291 3800
www.thompsonenamel.com

Allcraft Jewelry Supply Company
135 West 29th Street, Suite 402
New York, NY 10001
Tel: 1-800-645-7124
allcrafttools@yahoo.com
www.allcraftonline.com

Enamelwork Supply Company
1022 NE 68th Street
Seattle, WA 98115
Tel: 800-596-3257 or 206-525-9271
ewsco@comcast.net

Enamel Emporium
1221 Campbell Road
Houston, TX 77055
Tel: 713-984-0552

Welsh Products
PO Box 845
932 Grant Street
Benicia, CA 94510
www.welshproducts.com
Riso screens for thermal imagers,
ancillary printing equipment

Rio Gande
7500 Bluewater Road
Albuquerque, NM 87121
Tel: 800-545-6566
www.riogrande.com

USEFUL WEBSITES

• http://enews.heywoodenamels.com/
(Australian enameller, Alan Heywood)
• www.enamellers.nl/english/
(The Dutch Society of Enamellers)
• www.glass-on-metal.com
(Online enamel magazine)
• www.enamellers.org
(The British Society of Enamellers)
• www.cidae.com
(The Spanish Society of Enamellers)
• www.emaux-soyer.com
(French enamel manufacturer)
• www.goldman-enamel.com
(Dutch enameller and European supplier
of Thompson enamel, Ellen Goldman)
• www.studiofusiongallery.co.uk
(London Gallery specialising in
contemporary international enamel
jewellery, silver ware, and panels)
• www.metalcyberspace.com
• www.ajwells.co.uk
•www.smithmetal.com

BIBLIOGRAPHY

Ball, Fred; *Experimental Techniques in Enamelling*, Van Nostrand Reinhold Company, 1972

Brittain, A., and Morton, P.; *Engraving on Precious Metals*, NAG Press, 1958

Chamberlain, Walter; *Etching and Engraving*, Thames and Hudson, 1972/1984

Clarke, G. and Feher, F. and I.; *The Technique of Enamelling*, BT Batsford Ltd., 1988

Cockrell, Dorothy; *Beginner's Guide to Enamelling*, Search Press, 2004

Cohen, Karen L.; *The Art of Fine Enamelling*, Sterling Publishing Co. Inc., 2002

Darty, Linda; *The Art of Enamelling – Techniques, Projects and Inspirations*, Lark Books, 2004

Palmer, Denise; *New Crafts – Enamelling*, Lorenz Books, 1998

Seeler, Margaret; *Enamel Medium for Fine Art*, Dorrance Publishing Co., Inc., 1997

Speel, Erika; *The Dictionary of Enamelling – History and Techniques*, Ashgate, 1998

Speel, Erika; *Popular Enamelling*, BT Batsford Ltd., 1984

Strosahl, J.P., Strosahl, J.L., and Barnhart, C.L.; *A Manual of* Cloisonné *and* Champlevé, Thames and Hudson, 1982

Untracht, Oppi; *Enamelling on Metal*, Chilton Company, 1957/1962

Werge Hartley, Jeanne; *Enamelling on Precious Metals*, The Crowood Press, 2002

40/40 colour concepts. *Panel. Collaboration by Ruth Ball and Mary Brodie, 2004. Enamel, copper and textiles, 40 × 60 cm (15¾ × 23½ in.). Photo: Ruth Ball*

INDEX